YoungW

2004 POETRY CO

ONCE UPON A RHYME

IMAGINATION FOR
A NEW GENERATION

Poems From Cheshire
Edited by Steve Twelvetree

 Young**Writers**

First published in Great Britain in 2005 by:
Young Writers
Remus House
Coltsfoot Drive
Peterborough
PE2 9JX
Telephone: 01733 890066
Website: www.youngwriters.co.uk

SB ISBN 1 84460 665 1

Foreword

Young Writers was established in 1991 and has been passionately devoted to the promotion of reading and writing in children and young adults ever since. The quest continues today. Young Writers remains as committed to engendering the fostering of burgeoning poetic and literary talent as ever.

This year's Young Writers competition has proven as vibrant and dynamic as ever and we are delighted to present a showcase of the best poetry from across the UK. Each poem has been carefully selected from a wealth of *Once Upon A Rhyme* entries before ultimately being published in this, our twelfth primary school poetry series.

Once again, we have been supremely impressed by the overall high quality of the entries we have received. The imagination, energy and creativity which has gone into each young writer's entry made choosing the best poems a challenging and often difficult but ultimately hugely rewarding task - the general high standard of the work submitted amply vindicating this opportunity to bring their poetry to a larger appreciative audience.

We sincerely hope you are pleased with our final selection and that you will enjoy *Once Upon A Rhyme Poems From Cheshire* for many years to come.

Contents

Alistair Barnes (11)	69
Ross Wiggins (10) & Jordan Holland (11)	70
Raqim Mohammed (7)	70
Chris Johnson (7)	71
Charlotte Butler (7)	71
Alexander Beecroft (7)	72
Kieran Kenny (8)	72
Daniel Price (11)	73
Jack Griffiths (10)	73
Christopher Taylor & Luke Cartwright (10)	74
Fiona Farnsworth (10)	75
Gemma Clarke & Sally Hind (10)	76
Ella Callaghan Rhodes & Juliet Booth (10)	77
Jack Gilmartin & Alun Davies (10)	78
Emma Tyler & Daniela Taylor (10)	79

Lostock Hall Primary School

Holly Devereux (10)	79
Shelley Owen (10)	80
Emily Brennan (6)	81
Charlotte Brennan (10)	82
Leah Ward (10)	83
Katie Trollope (10)	83
Mia Lees (8)	84

Manor House Primary School

Michael James Thompson (9)	84
Oliver Thompson (10)	85
Tassha Jones (9)	85
Hazel Clarke (10)	86
Alex Jones (9)	86
Jade Ireland (11)	87
Matthew Furlong (10)	87
Erin Sykes (11)	88
Nic Simpkin (10)	88
Matthew Steele (11)	89
Matthew Dawson (10)	89
Lauren Oultram (10)	89
Jamie London (10)	90
Adam Reeves (11)	90
Mark Heighton (10)	91

Tom Halliwell (11)	91
Philip Sparke (10)	92
Thomas Stockton (10)	92
George McCormick (8)	93
Michael Nield (10)	93
Connor Karl Bladen (10)	94
Dominic Howard (9)	94
Daniel Mulhern (11)	95
Callum Howard (10)	95
Josh Slater (10)	96
Jennifer Owens (8)	96
Lauren Yarwood (9)	96
Steven Moores (9)	97
Georgia Merry (9)	97
Katherine Sparke (8)	98
Lauren Riddoch (10)	98
Lucy Ryder (9)	99
Lauren Furlong (9)	99
Lucy Mollat (9)	100
David Thompson (7)	100
Samantha Morgan (9)	100
Cecilia Vinchenzo (9)	101
Alice Harmer (10)	101
Madeleine Clarke (8)	102
Sophie Slater (10)	102
Pippa Webber (7)	103
Laura-Jane Garvie (9)	103

St Lewis' Primary School, Warrington

Zoe Isles (9)	103
Kathryn Gleave	104
Charlotte Woodall (9)	104
Aidan Nolan (9)	105
Olivia Quinn	105
James Gleave	105
Jessica Gorton	106
Lydia Smith (9)	106
Eleanor Vize (9)	107
Joseph Makin	107
Heather Morgan (9)	108
Shaun Irving (9)	108

St Vincent's RC Junior School, Altrincham

Wistaston Junior School

The Poems

The Nature Of Trees Alive

The leaves are waving
Song and soundly
The branches wave
The leaves come off
The roots come out of the ground
The roots begin to move
The leaves all fall off
And then the branches
Turn into woody arms and hands
And the two eyes made out of wood
Open.

Connor Scott Owen (5)

My Pet

My pet is cuddly and furry and it has long claws,
It has got very long whiskers,
It has got a very special bed.

When I come home from school, it wags its tail,
It runs around the chair and goes mad,
He brings his favourite teddy to me.

My dog is called Milo,
My dad thought of it.

My pet is really clumsy and bouncy
But I still love him.

He comes to me when I say his name,
He is a boxer dog.

Georgia Kirby (7)
Bredbury Green Primary School

Mystery On TV

Mystery, mystery always so strange,
People with guns all in range,
I feel excited as it begins to unfold,
Detectives are young,
Some are old.

I like using my brain on something hard,
That's why I like mysteries,
Sometimes they are histories.

Lieutenants creep around,
Stealthy,
Mostly they are healthy.

Some things are stolen,
Some people escape through a hole.

People break the law,
Sometimes they are sore.

Ben Pace (7)
Bredbury Green Primary School

I Went To A Football Match

I went to a football match
And Man U won on penalties,
I felt happy because
Man U are my favourite team in the whole world.

It tastes fresh
Like butterflies are in my belly.

When Man U scored I celebrated
And cheered
And I cheer the name of the player who scored.

Calum Cranwell (7)
Bredbury Green Primary School

My Pet

My pet is scruffy
And likes to go for walks,
I throw a ball for her to play with.

When I come in from school
She scratches me,
Then I play with her,
She does some tricks
And I give her a Snacko,
Her Snacko smells!

She lives in my house
And sleeps in a basket in my room,
Sometimes she is a little monkey,
Her name is Penny,
She is a cutie,
She is very playful.

Helena Bailey (7)
Bredbury Green Primary School

My Pet

It is furry, long and fluffy,
It moults a lot - on my hand, on my body,
It is friendly,
It scratches its cage and tries to get out when it sees me.

My pet is called Harvey,
My mum just thought of it,
He has sticky-up ears that lie down when I stroke him.

He sometimes goes to sleep on me,
My pet is white and grey,
He likes to run around in the garden,
My pet is a comfy pet,
My pet hugs me a lot,
I love my pet and I don't want him to ever die.

Megan Woodier (7)
Bredbury Green Primary School

My Pets

They open their mouths and make bubbles,
They have a little tail,
They like to swim around
In a tank,
I call them Sparkle and Sunshine,
Sparkle is orange and sparkly,
Sunshine is yellow and bright,
When we get to Nana's we feed them and
Clean the tank out,
The fish food smells!
They were only 99p each when we got them,
They tried to bite a hole in the bag,
They did bite a little hole,
But the water didn't come out!
We got home just in time.

I was excited when I was going to get my fish.

Kerys Heath (7)
Bredbury Green Primary School

My Pet

My pet looks like a snowball,
It likes running around in its hutch.

My pet lives in a cage,
It runs around in my arms.

My pet's name is Miffy,
The best thing I like doing with my pet
Is holding it,
It snuggles into me and hugs me.

It has long ears,
My pet eats Bunny mix,
I love my pet because it always hugs me.

Ruth Wallworth (7)
Bredbury Green Primary School

Scary Sleepover

It feels like . . .
They are going to get spooked
At any time!
An old mansion,
A few cobwebs,
The lights flash on and off,
When they get spooked,
I do!

I feel that the same things will happen to me,
I feel scared,
I hide behind a chair!

When they go on a challenge,
I cheer,
When they get lost,
I put my hands over my face,
I ask my mum if I can have a cushion,
I jump under my covers,
And bring the cushion with me.

It feels like I'm going to get pulled under the bed!

Andrew Lynam (7)
Bredbury Green Primary School

My Pet

My pet looks like a skinny sausage,
It is brown and it barks,
It likes to eat sausages and chocolate biscuits.

My pet likes to sleep on the chairs,
My mum shouts!

She likes to play football,
She dribbles it with her nose,
She supports Manchester City.

Kayla Myers (7)
Bredbury Green Primary School

Alton Towers

Spinball Whizzer is so much fun,
You go round and round,
And nearly upside down,
You bang your head on the back a lot
If you lean forward
But then the ride is virtually over.

Black Hole is very *cool!*
You go on a spiral up to the top,
When you're passing you see the Black Hole itself,
When you get to the top,
You fall   D
          O
            W
               N the hole.
You scream and scream and then it does it again
Until the ride is over.

On the Submission you go up and up
Until you go upside down,
The second time you just hang there,
If you have money in your pockets,
It just falls out.

Enterprise makes me feel sick!
You get inside the cart and go faster and faster,
Then you go up,
It's not like a Ferris wheel,
You go upside down.

Caitlin Taylor (7)
Bredbury Green Primary School

Football

Players shouting to each other,
Goalkeepers saving shots from the opposition,
Shouts and boos from the crowd.

Penalty
The player places the ball on the penalty spot,
The crowd keeps quiet,
They put their hands over their eyes,
They hold their breath and hope that they will score.
A goal!

The crowd cheer,
They sing,
They stand up and wave flags around.

Red card - a player gets pushed,
Someone gets thumped,
The referee gets a red card out of his pocket,
The player gets sent off,
He is sad,
He is angry,
The crowd shout, 'Get off.'

If I went I would cheer and be cheerful.

Oliver Saberton (7)
Bredbury Green Primary School

My Cat

My cat is ginger and white,
When it's hungry, it scratches at the wall,
It curls up like a bridge,
It scratched me on my head.

Jake Woodacre (7)
Bredbury Green Primary School

Football

When my favourite team scores I cheer,
When my unfavourite team score I go 'D'oh!'
I get excited when it is a corner to my favourite team.
When it is a penalty I say, 'Put it away!'

When we do a good tackle,
And the ref gives a free kick to them,
I feel angry,
I love it when the opposition get sent off!

If it is a free kick to my favourite team,
In a good position,
I go, 'Hit it in there!'

It tastes like chocolate chip cookies,
When my best football team scores,
It tastes like chocolate spread.

I feel great when my team win,
I feel sad when the other team win.

The atmosphere is great at the stadium,
It feels great to be there,
They all sing songs to boost the team up,
My team,
Manchester United.

Ben Mackintosh (7)
Bredbury Green Primary School

Being Poorly

I wish I was at school,
I'm getting bored at home,
I hope I get better soon,
And I'm not like this till next June,
Being poorly is just not cool,
I wish I was back at school.

Maya Robertson (7)
Bredbury Green Primary School

The Pet

It looks like cotton wool,
It likes playing,
It sleeps anywhere,
Its name is Max,
I play with it.

It likes eating chocolate chips,
It is furry,
It does not like going in a cage,
It hates big pets.

It likes scratching me,
When it hears food,
It charges at me,
It goes everywhere,
Sometimes it does not like me.

Zachary Abbott (7)
Bredbury Green Primary School

My Pet

It is like a ball of wool,
All fluffy,
My pet likes climbing on my bed,
It sleeps in my bed,
He curls up like a bridge.

His name is Tigger,
He looks like a tiger.

I play with my pet,
He chases his rattly ball,
He eats packet food,
Rabbit, game and duck!

My pet pooeed in my brother's shoe!
'That cat is annoying!' he said.

Shannon Walker (7)
Bredbury Green Primary School

My Pets

My pets are called Rosy and Rocky,
Rosy is yellow,
Rocky is black,
Rocky is deaf and he has a poorly leg,
Rocky can't hear when we call him,
He doesn't get lost,
Because he knows his way home,
Rocky is 112 in dog years,
He is an old dog,
Rosy is 60 in dog years.

I have a cat as well,
Called Trixie,
She likes to eat birds and rabbits,
I used to have a cat called Harry,
He was black and white and he died
Because of a poorliness.

Sam Caller (7)
Bredbury Green Primary School

The Football Match

I went to a football match,
Man U are going to win,
I feel happy because I know
Man U are *going* to win.

It feels like butterflies are in my belly,
Man U *are* going to win.

When my team score, I cheer
And shout for Rooney,
Man U are winning.

When their team fouls our team,
I shout 'Get off!'
Man U has won!

Jack Hutton (7)
Bredbury Green Primary School

My Dog

My dog bounces up and down
In my room,
It goes on my bed and scratches,
He sleeps in my room.

It does everything you say
If you drop anything
He will pick it up,
It eats dog food.

Jack Fawcett (7)
Bredbury Green Primary School

Poem About Iraq

Hostages are being taken
And never let go
Some are being beheaded
And some we don't know.

Weapons are being used
Like they are little toys
Blowing people up
Like they are a little insect.

All they want is money
So they blow up buildings
Don't care what happens
All they want is death.

People are innocent
Running away
International help coming over their way
Countries all against them
Everybody dying for a war.

Austin Brock-Clements (10)
Broadstone Hall Primary School

Poem About Iraq

In Iraq the conflict goes on and on,
The population goes down as time passes,
The terror grows as days go by,
And families' hearts are filled with dread!

The weapons that are meant to have caused it,
Do they exist, only they know it?
With grenades planted in every corner,
With tanks and missiles all exploding.

With innocent people being sent to fight,
All through the day and through the night,
Angry Americans want their revenge,
And fearless Iraqis won't let them have it.

Hussain was hiding in a hole,
While people die in fire and smoke,
With people providing him with food,
They should be ashamed, those helpless fools.

With people camping out in streets,
They won't last with them at their feet,
But won't get away with people lurking,
Who could they be, 'Hey, would you risk it?'

Robert McNair (10)
Broadstone Hall Primary School

Winter Poem

W hen the cold and frosty wind howls,
 I t feels like ice-cold fingers,
N ever missing a spot,
T rees are missing their dancing leaves,
E very time it gets colder, the trees are getting lonelier,
R ight on time the winter goes.

Naomi Lindop (10)
Broadstone Hall Primary School

Sad And Hatred

People dying,
Children crying,
Blood flying everywhere,
Machine guns punching,
Through the pouring rain,
Everybody's a target.

A bomb's just gone off,
Guts just flew everywhere,
People terrified,
Afraid it's going to happen to them.

Callum Kilburn (10)
Broadstone Hall Primary School

Haikus

A flower growing,
To be tall like other plants
It hangs while growing

It has no water
It's going to die hanging
I liked that flower.

Ellie Ralphs (8)
Broadstone Hall Primary School

Winter Poem

Winter is a large white coat on the ground,
White as white and shivering of the cold breath of wind.

The cold frost was gripping me in its freezing hands,
The trees were dancing in the lonely wind.

The snow falls pathetically from the sky
Like someone crying,
Identical to when the cold ice melts.

Sam Gilluley (10)
Broadstone Hall Primary School

Queen Swan - Haikus

Massive white wings spread
Drifting down to the water
Ripples disappear.

Showing off her wings,
Ducking under clear water,
Turning upside down.

Olivia Cooper (8)
Broadstone Hall Primary School

Terror In Iraq

Car bombs, ranting and raving,
Frightened people killed because of those monstrous things,
Hostages taken just to stop the violence,
Innocent people captured and fear for their lives.

Missiles launched out of nowhere,
No intended target, just hoping it will hit something,
Hitting innocent buildings and people,
Causing war, destruction - *bang!*

Jamie McQuillan (10)
Broadstone Hall Primary School

My Brother's Birth - Haikus

I felt it inside
He started to cry for Mum
Small trembling body
Smiling happily
He lay there looking at me
Relying on me.

Emmily Albiston (8)
Broadstone Hall Primary School

A Nonsense Poem

(A Shakespearean poem)

Shall I compare thee with the stars above?
If thou come we will make true love so much,
Thou feel like a touch of a bright dove,
I get so amazed when our fingers touch,
Though hast smooth arms that feel so relaxing,
I will take thee on a show and then bow.
When we play tig I feel like collapsing.
Your nose is so plump I can feel it now.
Thou smells like the scent of a bright red rose.
I will bring thee thou breakfast on a tray.
I will do you a really good strong pose.
I will take thee to the ash bar all day.
I've got some powder so we can bake.
I hope you enjoy your delicious cake.

Jessica Reeves (9)
Broadstone Hall Primary School

A Nonsense Sonnet

(A Shakespearean Poem)

Shall I compare thee with a summer's day?
If thou come we'll make true love so happy.
Will you come with me to a Shakespeare play?
Do you like me? I'm a happy chappy.
Thou art so sexy you drive me crazy.
If thee want we'll have a happy marriage.
Will you still love me if I am lazy?
If thee want I will give you a carriage.
Your skin is so soft like a dove.
Tonight I will give you a big red rose.
This marriage is so happy, it is love.
For you to smell with your little cute nose.
Our happy marriage has been divine,
So would you like to come wine and dine?

Emily Furber (9)
Broadstone Hall Primary School

Rain - Kennings

Wet bringer
Gutter flower
Pavement jumper
Plant grower.

Animal wetter
Pavement leaper
Drink maker
Paper seeper.

Slip slider
Bored bringer
Window runner
Drain singer.

Life saver
Sad maker
Umbrella opener
Puddle maker.

Adam Barrow (8)
Broadstone Hall Primary School

The Weather

The ever-changing weather can be angry and happy,
When a horrific hurricane occurs,
The speed is like a racing car in a national race.

When it is sunny,
The beaming sun is waving and giving
You some love, just where you need it.

But when it is hailing,
The ugly hail is picking up some freezing ice
And throwing it at you, in your warm coat.

Emma Dickinson (10)
Broadstone Hall Primary School

A Nonsense Sonnet

(A Shakespearean Poem)

Shall I compare thee to the best reward?
I can run thee a nice hot bubbly bath,
I hope you will never ever, ever be bored!
Thee will walk through the romantic love path,
Your eyes are as blue as the sky itself,
People may think thee are stupid, you're not,
Your ears are as big as a baby elf,
Your baby will love his big blue wood cot,
Love hearts round the glowing room fills with joy,
Thee will have a magnificent baby,
I promise I will not be like Henry,
I will always have lots of faith in you,
Thee will love thy place we live in for years,
I was only kidding about those big ears.

Christopher Hall (9)
Broadstone Hall Primary School

Stranger Danger Beware!

Happy children holding hands
Beware!
Don't talk to strangers
Man staring
Out of the car window
Staring at the children
Beware!
Don't talk to strangers
Screaming
Trying
To run!
Oh no!
He is chasing us!

Chloe Manners-Jones (9)
Broadstone Hall Primary School

Terrified Guns

Frightened people they will lie,
Dreaming about the future,
Hoping that people won't cry,
But now they are left with a question, why?

Some rich, some poor,
Some wishing they had more,
Everything is so manic,
Who knows what will happen,
Nobody wants it to end in a panic,
It's all happening so quickly.

Machine gun,
Shoots for fun,
As people run,
The innocent lives are in other's hands.

Amie-Erika Hughes (10)
Broadstone Hall Primary School

Hostages

Hostages released or beheaded,
The hostage takers decide,
Decide on their full stop,
Or to carry on the sentence,
Killed or alive,
You are lucky with either,
The angry monsters,
Lurk in deep dark corners,
To perform deep dark deeds,
Innocent or not,
They still will take you,
Hostages can only wait,
Wait for the answer of death or life.

Leah Hartley (10)
Broadstone Hall Primary School

Iraq War

A war-torn place, holding its head in its hands,
No weapons were found, but still the war goes on,
Innocent people killed for no reason,
Happiness is a dream for them,
But a long way off it seems.

The leader of Iraq has gone,
But still the horror goes on,
Bloodthirsty men, taking hostages,
Nightmares you can't imagine,
One day they will be released,
But when, I'm not too sure.

People screaming as they hear the guns go,
Living in fear because terror is near,
The war is turning their lives to misery,
Angry, worried, frightened,
No one there to help them.

Matthew Goldsworthy (10)
Broadstone Hall Primary School

Poem

Bombs going off 24/7
Thousands of people dying all the time
People being held hostage,
Being beheaded.

People are dying, for no reason
Young kids about 10 fighting for their country
People praying for peace and happiness
Little kids and old people who are completely innocent.

People are panicking
Big tanks, cars and
Buildings blowing up.

Jake McDaid (10)
Broadstone Hall Primary School

Winter's Hand

Winter is an icy white hand,
Grabbing all the lonely trees.

Winter is a big white man sleeping on the land,
The ice is crying,
The trees are dying.

The icy white hand has grabbed me.

The man stood up and shook,
The trees came alive,
The ice flowed away.
And the icy white hand released me.

Matthew Worsley (10)
Broadstone Hall Primary School

The Monster

His eyes are blood-red,
He's hiding in my shed,
Or even under my bed,
I can't get him out of my head!

His claws are as sharp as knives,
He gets his prey just like an owl,
He gets up high and dives,
He even got a cat one day and
Scared him away with his nine lives.

His body is slimy like a slug,
That's why no one wants to give him a hug,
He gets into your mind just like a bug,
You want to give your eyes,
A pull and a tug.

He is as tall as a hurricane,
He needs a bit of a tame,
Because right now he'd put you
Through some pain!

Alexander John Taylor (10)
Brow CP School

Ghosts And Ghouls

Ghosts and ghouls
That give pity on fools,
Moving as fast as light,
To give you a fright.
Wizards and witches
On football pitches,
Ringing church bells
And casting all kinds of spells.
The beast they call Nasty Gnore
Burning dragons to make his pork,
It's not very nice
When he eats them with rice,
Next up is the invisible man,
He is always hitching a plan,
He is an incredible kind who
For all you know, is right behind you.
All these beasts are nasty not nice,
I would be surprised if they all didn't have lice,
The one I hate is the mountain yeti,
Other beasts call him Betty,
Ghosts and ghouls
That give pity on fools.

Alex Brown (10)
Brow CP School

The Storm

The furious old man roars at the top of his voice,
His fiery walking stick flying through the air,
His dark grey hair burdens the land,
His icy hands grab the house,
Like a snake wrapping around its victim,
The man's tears beat furiously against the window,
As he walks away, all is quiet.

James Duffy (10)
Brow CP School

The Houses On 51st Estate

Number 5 is a stout old lady,
With cracks in her face but twinkling eyes,
Sprawling comfortably and wearing her bright
Coloured beads with pride.

Number 7 is a thin young man,
Has a good job and is very smart,
Tall and proud looking down at all the peasants,
Smiling happily at the sun.

Number 9 and 11 are two young twins,
Being looked after by the elders,
Their eyes sparkling and glistening in the sun.

Number 13 is a tall spooky man who doesn't talk much,
He's big and bold and only has one eye,
This number has lost most of his hair and feels very wet inside.

Number 4 is a small and thin teenager putting music
On every night until 4 o'clock in the morning,
She is very unwanted in the street and she
Also has writing and pictures all over her face.

Lauren Swinney (10)
Brow CP School

The Dragonfly

Flying as noisy as a dragon, when he is hungry at night,
He is as long as a very long worm,
He moves as slowly as a running spider when it is frightened,
They dance with the fireflies at night,
Lives as a waterhog in the jungle,
Wings as sharp as an arrow,
Eyes as black as the darkest corner.

Adam Elwell (10)
Brow CP School

The Naughty House

A rich young man who likes to
Tease his neighbours a lot
And no one likes him
And everyone is fed up with him,
He wears a green coat with white stripes on it,
He plays with his toy cars
And tidies them up when he's done with them,
He watches out for his new neighbour,
He thinks about playing a trick on him
But he gets caught,
His new neighbour told him off,
He asked if he knew what he was doing,
He said, 'No' and ran off,
So his neighbours decided to play a trick on him,
Their plan had worked,
So the house said he was sorry,
They forgave him,
They were very happy forever
And he never played a trick again.

Georgina Cuthbert (10)
Brow CP School

The Butterfly

The butterfly is graceful and beautiful,
Dancing around the summer flowers,
She moves as slowly as she can,
Gliding through the air like a bird flapping her wings,
Her body is long and thin, like a petal on a daisy,
Her legs are tiny, like two pins,
Her eyes are as big as a lead on a pencil,
The butterfly is as quiet as a mouse.

Courtney Fairclough (10)
Brow CP School

Rainbows

The colours I see,
So beautiful to me,
All mixed together,
It's a phenomenal creation of the weather.

On rainy days they appear,
You only see them, never do you hear,
Unleashed by the cold, wet rain,
They relieve the world of its pain.

When it rains on the sun,
It takes away our games and fun,
We then leave our games,
While the rain puts out the
Sun's wonderful flames.

Once the sun has once again begun,
All of us go out and continue our fun,
Rain will return soon again,
To haunt women, children and even men.

Lorna Costello (10)
Brow CP School

The Dragonfly

He is as big as a big spider,
He is as fat as a cheetah,
He lives in a hole that is as black
As a mole and as big as a house
But as thin as a pin.
He loves to eat, loves to gag,
But the funny old thing
Will never give a thing.

Michael Owens (10)
Brow CP School

A Hedgehog

A hedgehog is as prickly as a thorn bush,
When I see a girl I blush,
I can roll up in a ball,
I can get really small,
I live with my mum and dad,
I am named after the England flag,
A hedgehog smart as a human being,
I'm glad my brain can fit in,
I may look fat,
But I am very fast,
My friends might look weird,
But at least I've got a beard,
When I'm out in the forest,
I only hang around,
I am trying to do a band,
But I've only got one drum stand.

Daniel Sullivan (10)
Brow CP School

The Dragonfly

The dragonfly cuts the air like lightning,
The dragonfly hovers like a flying saucer,
It is a shooting bullet,
And is an engine in a rally car,
And its wings are fanning feathers,
The body is a big stick,
And the eyes are shiny gems,
In 30 seconds it will be far,
They blast in the night,
In the day it will be May,
At night they are at bay,
When they are alone, they will moan!

Adam Goulbourn (10)
Brow CP School

Weather

The storm is like an old grumpy man,
And if he sees you on his garden,
He launches his walking stick at you
And when his thunderous voice shouts
The wind shrieks like his pet bulldog,
Across the other side of the country,
There is a lovely beach,
It makes you take off all your clothes,
And go to get an ice cream,
To cool you down,
Then go back to build sandcastles,
Then bury yourself from head to toe,
And eat your luxurious picnic,
When you've had a great fun day,
You go home to watch TV,
Then you go to bed,
To bed to have a good night's sleep.

Chris Hough (10)
Brow CP School

The Sun

This person is a happy clown
That only appears at circuses and parties,
He wears a bright orange nose with blond hair and
Wears blue clothing and wears a white bow tie
And makes you happy,
Sometimes when he is putting on a show for you
He squirts you with his bottle of water,
If he ever offers you a grey box,
It might have a toy snake inside,
He pulls from under his velvet soft sleeve
A long stream of green ribbon,
Like I's lined up straight,
So remember to be careful around clowns.

Steven Stoba (11)
Brow CP School

The Fierce Windy Storm

The storm rages loudly but sounds like a fierce, selfish giant,
Flickering in the sky, the lightning bolt rushes and hurdles down,
Then its thunderous voices echo and sound scary.
The wind shrieks loudly like a lion's roar,
Screeching and making trees shake,
The wind goes calm, then fierce again but the only one
Who stands outside finds that it will get colder and colder.
Icy grips grab and hold the houses,
Like a crocodile's sharp teeth and big jaws.
So when the crocodile grips your house, don't panic,
When the rain beats angrily against the windowpanes,
Shouting 'Let me in, I want to make you wet.'
When you are inside,
The coal fire will keep you warm,
Then you are as warm as a blanket.

Danielle Cohen (10)
Brow CP School

Christopher Hough

Great at football,
Playing for Man City,
Friends with everyone he meets,
He's very friendly in school,
He gets A's in maths,
He gets A's in English,
A's on in science,
And even A's in PE,
By now you must know who
I'm talking about,
Yes now you have got it,
Because it is Christopher Hough.

Jack Swinney (10)
Brow CP School

The Butterfly

A butterfly moves very swiftly
Through the bright blue sky.
All the colours changing in the sky.
The colours are black and
Yellow and brown
And light and dark blue and pink.
The antenna long and thin and brown,
And all shapes changing in the breeze,
With all shapes and sizes on them
And the butterfly looks down.
He can see towns and villages under him.
When he lands back home,
He lies down on a leaf and dozes off
Then he wakes up and flutters off.

Bethany Cuthbert (10)
Brow CP School

A Day On The Beach

On a hot summer's day,
I stretched out in the shade after a sleep,
I got up and ran down to the sea.

When I got there, the waves welcomed me,
Like I was one of them,
I splashed about like a whale.

But the sand covered my feet like snakes,
So I ran as fast as a cheetah,
To where I was sleeping before.

I got my things and went home,
Where it was safe from the sand.

Ryan Taylor (10)
Brow CP School

The Rainforest

The colours I see fascinate me,
The sounds all around me make me smile,
I've seen loads of creatures and a crocodile,
The taste of bananas brighter than the sun,
I can't believe the things I've done,
There's Mrs Ed
She's newly wed,
Mr Parrot is big and bold,
He has many great stories to be told,
Mr Ape has seen the world,
He brushed his hair until it curled,
There's a rascal, a real baboon,
He eats his breakfast, without a spoon,
Then there's Lion, a great king,
He can roar better than anything,
Loud by day, silent by night,
When they wake up they look a sight,
At midnight, there's not a peep,
So when they nap, it's a pleasant sleep.

Sally Houghton (10)
Brow CP School

Houses

Looking down at the other houses,
We're looking down at the other houses,
At the side of us with clean sparkling eyes,
With little cars scattered all over the place on the drive,
Flowers planted all around the house like a border,
Wearing a golden cloak like a magician,
The door like an opening mouth,
Eyes opening to a fresh morning sun.

Amy Sears (10)
Brow CP School

Dragons

Fire blasting lizards flying through the night,
When they're through the clouds, they are out of sight,
They blast their prey with blazing fire,
Then bring it back to their lair to admire,
They eat the meat off their bones,
And rope it off where nobody goes,
Knights try and slay these beasts,
They celebrate with a royal feast.

The dragons protect their little eggs,
Before they grow their arms and legs,
When they finally breathe fire,
They bring their own prey to admire,
When they are fully grown,
They will cause terror on their own.

Jordan Gillespie (10)
Brow CP School

Whining Witches

A huddle of witches all cackling loudly,
Like monkeys in the zoo when they haven't had their bananas,
They are as wicked as cats chasing terrified mice,
As frightening as a lion roaring at his dinner,
They're as bossy as a huge fire-breathing dragon,
Even their black cats are as fierce as a panther,
Their cauldrons swing from side to side,
As black as a bat flying through the night sky,
As the sun slowly sets,
It is time for them to leave,
But when the moon shines over the Earth,
They will be back to cause trouble.

Conor Hatton (10)
Brow CP School

Chocolate

Warm, melting, tastes delicious,
Luxury, the food of kings, yummy!
The taste is so magnificent,
When I eat this one it'll be my 600th.

Melt it, freeze it, boil it, bake it,
Microwave it if you like!
But if you eat it like that
You'll be here all night!
Grr! All this talking's making me hungry!

Garlic bread, crackers and meat,
Chocolate with that is always a treat!
So lick your lips, take in the delight!
Cos if you don't you'll be here all night!

If you don't like chocolate well that's just fine,
Cos in my eyes, it's simply divine!
And if you don't like chocolate well that's just bad,
Simply because you're blinking mad!

Now here's the epilogue so listen up!
I'm gonna go get myself some chocolate grub!
Now *if* you haven't tried it,
Some is in your nearest shop
It's only 30p . . .
So, go and get some!

Naomi Hunt (10)
Brow CP School

Untitled

My brother feels like a fish,
My brother smells like the sea,
My brother looks like a fish,
My brother tastes disgusting.

Ria Hill (7)
Bruntwood Primary School

Quickly

Quickly goes the roundabout,
Quickly goes the roller skates,
Quickly the people drink the cola,
Quickly goes the fireworks.

Quickly the rocket took off,
Quickly the girl got her money
From her pocket and bought a golden locket.
Quickly the wind whistled around the roller coasters
But the quickest is the cheetah's run and
The horse's gallop!

Becki Phillips (9)
Bruntwood Primary School

Quickly

Quickly the cheetah went past,
With legs that made him go so fast,
Quickly the flames of fire get higher and higher.

Quickly the rain came down,
Quickly the bike came into town,
Quickly the ice froze the lake,
Quickly lots of people came to take some cake.

Quickly the boy bounced the ball,
But quickest of all, the cat jumped off the wall.

Georgina Cornes (8)
Bruntwood Primary School

Fox

My fox feels like a soft cat,
My fox smells like flowers,
My fox looks like a wolf,
My fox tastes like a fish.

Hannah May Massey (9)
Bruntwood Primary School

Quickly

Quickly is a motorbike.
Quickly is an Olympic runner called Mike
Quickly is a bird's wing
One of the birds that likes to sing.

Quickly is an aeroplane flying past
Quickly is a leopard running fast
Quickly is a roller coaster going down the slope
Quickly is a drink going down a throat.

Quickly is a secretary writing fast
But the quickest thing of all is a rapper singing their song,
Now that's a blast!

Alicia Whyatt (8)
Bruntwood Primary School

Mum

My mum smells like nothing,
My mum looks like a fairy,
My mum feels like a soft teddy,
My mum tastes like ice cream,
My mum sounds like loud thunder.

Charlotte Tooley (6)
Bruntwood Primary School

Mum

My mum smells like pink flowers,
My mum looks like a beautiful queen,
My mum feels like soft feathers,
My mum tastes like chocolate biscuits,
My mum sounds like a quiet mouse.

Kenan Plant (6)
Bruntwood Primary School

Kennings Cat

A bin scrounger
A sofa lounger
A sun bather
A milk craver
A scary hisser
A cute lisper
An indigo colour
A string puller
A body spinner
Hell's dinner!

Lily McCormick (10)
Bruntwood Primary School

Autumn

A utumn is a damp and cold season
U sually hedgehogs hibernate in the autumn
T he leaves twirl into mould,
U sually the leaves come off the trees,
M any colours are in the autumn like red and brown,
N o sun in autumn.

Aimee Morgan (7)
Bruntwood Primary School

Grandma

My grandma smells like toothpaste,
My grandma looks like a queen,
My grandma feels like a kiss,
My grandma tastes like nice apples,
My grandma sounds like a teacher.

Thomas Lloyd-Smith (5)
Bruntwood Primary School

Sun And The Moon

If only, if only the sun shone
no reply reflecting the moon
and all that's gone by.

Anger, as red as a volcano
is separating them.

The anxious white moon is hiding, shy.
The red-hot sun is trying not to pass by.

Fear and fright is separating them,
Let's just hope they don't lie.

Mazen Abdul-Latif (10)
Bruntwood Primary School

Love Is A Heart Beating

Love is there and love is everywhere,
Love is like a warm bed
Love is like a boat, floating on a calm sea.

Love is like a big bear hug
Love is like a big sloppy kiss from your dog,
Love is like drinking a hot pot of cocoa.
Love is like sitting by a hot fire.

Rosemarie Hill (10) & Ria Hill
Bruntwood Primary School

My Dog

My dog smells like bad breath,
My dog looks like a sheepdog,
My dog feels like a blanket,
My dog tastes like chicken bones,
My dog sounds like a wolf.

Jake Giles (6)
Bruntwood Primary School

Quickly

Quickly the cheetah gets its prey.
Quickly Rooney runs out to play.
Quickly the ice freezes.
Quickly the wind breezes.
Quickly the fire burns the house.
Quickly the owl chases a mouse.
Quickly the motorbike speeds downtown.
Quickly the butterfly spins round and round.
Quick is the shark - but quickest of all
Is Wayne Rooney on the ball.

Jake Stoba (8)
Bruntwood Primary School

Quickly

Quickly I drove the bumper car.
Quickly the man went on his motorbike.
Quickly I ran around.
Quickly I got dressed.
Quickly the plane took off.
Quickly the train went to London.
Quickly the dog ran after the cat.

Nico Jackson (10)
Bruntwood Primary School

Autumn Is . . .

Autumn is a damp season when leaves fall off the trees,
Autumn is a damp season when the weather is cold,
Autumn is a damp season with colours of orange and yellow,
Autumn is a damp season so the birds fly south.

Dylan Daniels (8)
Bruntwood Primary School

My Magic Box

(Inspired by 'Magic Box' by Kit Wright)

In my magic box . . .
I found a snapping shark and a smiling snake,
I found a bleating bear and a bowling bubble,
I found a teleporting tank and a talking tiger.
I found a poorly python and a playful poltergeist.
I found a bashful black adder and a biodegradable bat.
I found a cheating cheetah and a calling cat.
I found a heated hat and a horrified horse.
I found a kneeling koala and a kick-boxing kangaroo.

Matthew Kitcher (10)
Bruntwood Primary School

Limerick

There once was a woman called Elaine,
Who was in such terrible pain,
She bumped her leg,
On a peg,
And never felt the same again.

There once was a woman from Leeds,
Who swallowed a bucket of seeds,
And in an hour, she turned into a flower,
And around her was loads of weeds.

Bethan Bergin-Rooney (10)
Bruntwood Primary School

Autumn

A utumn is cold and damp,
U nder the clouds, the leaves
T wirl to the ground,
U sually very, very cold,
M ouldy leaves rot
N obody goes outside.

Luke Bergin-Rooney (7)
Bruntwood Primary School

Kennings Kitten

Mother - seeker
Milk - drinker
String - player
Cute - cuddler
Chair - sleeper
Wallpaper - scratcher
Chicken - eater
Fire - liker
High - pouncer.

Samantha Calder (10)
Bruntwood Primary School

Kennings Big Foot

Forest prowler
Ground shaker
Man seeker
Human eater
Woolly fur
Sharp teeth
Big eyes
Heavy feet.

Alex Northey (10)
Bruntwood Primary School

Autumn

A utumn is damp and wet,
U nfortunately autumn is not sunny,
T here is Hallowe'en, harvest and lots of coats,
U nfortunately there are no birds because they
M igrate to hot places,
N o sun in autumn.

James Dickinson (7)
Bruntwood Primary School

Magic Box

(Inspired by 'Magic Box' by Kit Wright)

In my magic box I found . . .
An aggressive ant and a
Appalling antelope.

I found a bashful bear
And a big, blue, bouncy bubble.

I found a crunching, crushing,
Crocodile and a colourful
Curious cat.

I found a dim-witted duck,
And a disco dancing dragon.

I found an enormous, elegant,
Elephant and an electric,
Egg-eating eel.

I found a fabulous family,
Of flamingos and a
Fantastic fearless frog.

I found a grotesque, gruesome
Gherkin and a grumpy, grey-haired
Grandma.

I found a horrifying hairy hyena and
A humble honest hippo.

I found an irresistible incredible ice
Cream and an important indigo insect.

Laura Carruthers (10)
Bruntwood Primary School

Fish

My fish feels like a rose,
My fish smells like a catfish,
My fish looks like a catfish,
My fish tastes like a cat.

Emily Giles (7)
Bruntwood Primary School

My Magic Box
(Inspired by 'Magic Box' by Kit Wright)

In my magic box . . .
I found a singing sock and a snail snoring.
I found a karate-chopping koala and a kind-hearted kipper.
I found a crumpled carpet and a car, creating crumpets.
I found a pestering parrot and a partying pigeon.
I found a flying football and a fidgety fish.
I found an ordinary octopus and an original orange.
I found a dancing deer and a diving dolphin.
I found an awesome angel and an amazing apple.
I found a bellowing bull and a banging bell.
I found a laughing ladybird and a lazy leopard.
I found a hippy hedgehog and a hopping hyena
I found a gruesome gorilla and a grizzling grape.

Rose Evans (10)
Bruntwood Primary School

Untitled

When the wind is howling between the buildings
it is a wolf, searching for its lost cubs.
When the wind is whispering through the trees,
it is a snake slithering through the misty leaves.
When the wind is making a cold draught in the house,
it is an eagle swirling round, waiting to swoop on its prey.
When the wind is a flickering flame in a fire,
it is a dragon breathing smoky fire, creeping across the floor.
When the wind is a roaring lion calling for its mate.
When the wind is carrying a dandelion seed along,
it is a bumblebee buzzing through the air to a sweet smelling flower.
When the wind is breaking branches off a tree
it is a panda stomping along the grass, looking
for more leaves to eat.

Jade Latham (10)
Bruntwood Primary School

Limericks

There once was a man from Spain
Who had a peculiar pain
He sat in his car,
Drove really far,
And he never complained again.

There once was a woman from France
Who did a brilliant dance,
She went to a class,
Broke some glass,
And never got given a chance.

There once was a woman from Maine
Who liked to travel by plane,
She wanted to drive,
But decided to dive,
And she never drove again.

Lauren Evans (10)
Bruntwood Primary School

Kennings Dog

A hairy prowler
A cat fighter
A kennel dweller
A loud growler
A meat smeller
A tail wagger
A ball chaser
A stick fetcher
A bone chewer
A lead wearer
A face licker
A sloppy kisser
A wet nose.

Madia Choudhry (10)
Bruntwood Primary School

Feelings

Anger is red like
a fire is burning
and a volcano exploding.

Happiness is yellow like
a shiny sun in the sky
and a shiny yellow car.

Sadness is blue like
a tulip dying and a
blue flag waving and breaking.

Maleehah Choudhry (7)
Bruntwood Primary School

Quickly

Quickly the man moves out of the house,
Quickly the leaves fall off a tree,
Quickly we see,
Quickly the skateboard moves on the track.

Quickly the cheetah runs on a mat,
Quickly we make the buns on a tray,
Quick is a shark - but quickest of all
Is a hurricane starting to fall.

Hannah Kitcher (8)
Bruntwood Primary School

Untitled

When the wind is howling between the buildings,
it is a crying coyote.

When the wind is whispering through the trees,
it is a wolf charging on autumn leaves.

When the wind is making a cold draught in the house,
it is a lion yawning.

Jonathan Leatherbarrow (10)
Bruntwood Primary School

Quickly

Quickly a dog chases the cat.
Quickly a man sat.
Quickly a plane rushes over.
Quickly a cheetah gets its prey.

Quickly a boy ran round the playground.
Quickly a ball rolls away.
Quickly the time passes by.
Quickly the flames catch.

But quickest of all is the cheetah getting its prey.

Elena Newiss (8)
Bruntwood Primary School

Quickly

Quickly a tiger gets its prey.
Quickly a boy gets his ball.
Quickly a ball bounces up and down.
Quickly a boy runs round and round.

Quickly I saw a little gold locket.
Quickly a rocket shot up in the sky.
Quickly a girl went round with a rake,
But quickest of all, the little brown deer
As it runs round the field.

Emma Saxton (8)
Bruntwood Primary School

Quickly

Quickly the blood runs down my veins
Quickly my mind goes side to side
Quickly the fire goes down my pliers
Quickly the thunder goes under my chair
Quickly time goes down my spine.

Rhys Bateman (8)
Bruntwood Primary School

Quickly

Quickly the cat chased a bat.
Quickly the bird chased a worm.
Quickly the man ran out of the house.
Quickly the elephant stood on a mouse.

Quickly the boy played with the ball.
Quickly the girl ran out of the hall.
Quick was a bat who ran out of a hat,
But the quickest of them all was a cheetah
Who ran a mile away.

Lana Ali (8)
Bruntwood Primary School

My Family

Sometimes I love my mum
Sometimes I love my dad
Sometimes I love my sister
But do they love me?
My dad hates me so much
He forces me up the tree.

My baby sister is a crybaby
She always asks for a pick-up
Her nails are so sharp
I'm all covered in cuts.

My big sister is so bossy
She bosses me all around
And if I am a little cheeky
She'd beat me to the ground.

And did I say sometimes I love my mum?
I love her all the time
She's the best person in my life
And she'll always be mine.

Asha Blake (8)
Cloverlea Primary School

Emma

I am . . .

E xcellent and good
M ad but fun
M uch liked
A ngry like a devil.

T ire people out
H elpful and good
O n and off
M ad and funny
S oft and warm
O bedient and great
N ice and smart!

Emma Thomson (8)
Cloverlea Primary School

My Family Poem

My sister is eleven
Last year I was seven
I used to wear a nappy
But now I'm very happy

B rilliant
E xcellent
N ice

Jolly.

Ben Jackson (8)
Cloverlea Primary School

My Family

I really love my mother,
I really hate my brother,
But when my dad thinks I'm bad,
I get very, very sad.

I'm always arguing with my sister,
I laughed when her shoes gave her a blister,
My tiny baby sister is so cute,
But sometimes she can be a little brute.

Leila Djennati
Cloverlea Primary School

Harriet

I am . . .

H appy
A nd
R eal.
R easonably
I ntelligent
E xcited and
T empted.

Harriet Landsborough (8)
Cloverlea Primary School

The Ocean

The waves are like white galloping stallions
Jumping over the waves like jumping fish
With somebody on the back of them.

Rushing, crashing on the rocks,
Exploding like a bomb.

Matthew Rhodes (9)
Elworth Hall Primary School

River

The river is like the fast flowing waves
Bubbling all day long.
It trickles and ripples and flows as it goes.
It splashes like a tap dripping.
The water is as clear as crystal
And it shimmers all day long.
It is silky soft and smooth,
It is a sofa in the early morning sunrise,
Bright and clear.

Kate Highfield (9)
Elworth Hall Primary School

The Rain

On a rainy, rainy day, I come out to play
in the puddles.
Splish, splash, splosh, the sound of people
splashing in me.
I get bigger when it starts to rain
when it stops I shrivel up.

Nicholas Sparkes (9)
Elworth Hall Primary School

The Waves

The waves crash against the rocks
Then there is a treasure box
Floating on top
The waves look like a giant hand
The waves go over the sand
The waves roar in the air
Lots of people like to stare.

Aimee Bendall (9)
Elworth Hall Primary School

A Waterfall

Gushing waves rippling down like pure white stallions,
Galloping over the shelly golden beach,
Sparkling water trickling, trickling, trickling down,
And you can hear crashing waves bouncing off rocks,
Drip-drop, drip-drop,
But when water's dried up, everything stops.

Just like the clear blue sky,
A roaring lion in rain,
Or a big fat giant in the clouds in pain.

Bubbling water splashing all day,
Little kids always come out to play,
Splashing and playing, trickling as well,
Gushing, rippling, bouncing, crashing,
Drip-drop, drip-drop
But when water's dried up, everything stops!

Becci Scott (9)
Elworth Hall Primary School

Waterfall

The water is a monster roaring loudly
Crashing against the rock like a hammer.
Falling leaves from trees.
The bubbles pop as they drop.

The water is a monster roaring loudly
Splashing down onto people.
Sounds like thunder hitting the wall.
People screaming as it comes.

The water is a monster roaring loudly
Crashing down as loud as it can.
It will never stop
But will always drop.

Carrie May Smith (9)
Elworth Hall Primary School

Slipping River

The river is rippling silk
Gently waving around
The river is a piece of paper
Not making a sound.

The river is a piece of glass
Reflecting golden sunlight
Going round the corners
Getting in a fight.

The river is a slithering snake
Thinking of some trouble to make
It never wants to be big
It never wants to be a lake.

The river is an iceberg
Slipping up and down
It is as cold as the Atlantic sea
You don't want to drown.

Natalie Mason (9)
Elworth Hall Primary School

The Tidal Wave

It is instant mash, growing like mad,
It is a robber big and bad,
It is a giant, huge and loud,
It is a monster, roaring and proud,
It looks like a person stretching around,
It looks like a dragon, making lots of sound.

It sounds like a hairdryer, on at full speed,
It's a bit like a devil, doing a bad deed,
It is a pair of eyes, staring you down,
It is a madman, making you drown,
It is a washing machine, spinning and quick,
It is a tongue, not trying to lick.

Calum Elder (9)
Elworth Hall Primary School

Puddles

Drip-drop, drip-drop
Shining, making puddles a lot.
Sometimes it goes down the drain,
Or sometimes rain's a pain.

Puddles are like a tiny pool,
Sometimes puddles are at school,
Other times they're just for fun,
Or sometimes you get in trouble with your mum.

Puddles shine, puddles shimmer,
Puddles sparkle, puddles glimmer.
Puddles are like good babies
But swimming pools are glamorous ladies.

Puddles are like a tiny pool,
Sometimes puddles are at school,
Other times they're just for fun,
Or sometimes you get in trouble with your mum.

Puddles are splash zones
And when you hear your mum's moans
You know that you have to go in
And all that puddle fun has gone in the bin.

Puddles are like a tiny pool,
Sometimes puddles are at school,
Other times they're just for fun,
Or sometimes you get in trouble with your mum.

Sophie Hindley (9)
Elworth Hall Primary School

Streams

Streams are like see-through glass
With fish like sparkling bass,
Streams are snakes slithering through the country,
Streams twist and bend until the end,
Water helps fish breathe until they leave.

Alex Wilding (9)
Elworth Hall Primary School

The Ocean

The waves are big like
Horses and carts,
They will have top marks.

The fisherman wants to catch,
They will be on boats and
They will be using floats.

There are lots of dancing fish,
Watch out in case they
Dance on your dish!

Rhys Dolman (10)
Elworth Hall Primary School

Water

Water falls on the ground
as it makes a drip-drop sound.
Water is a glowing crystal
shimmering and shining in the sun.
Water flows slowly on the river bank,
I skimmed a stone, it bounced and sank!

Danny Rance (9)
Elworth Hall Primary School

The Big Wave

The wave is like one big dolphin,
Jumping out of the water,
Tiny little bubbles bubbling up shiny white water,
Crashing against the rocks,
Like one big footstep from a giant,
It is like watching one big race.

Charlie Nash (10)
Elworth Hall Primary School

Rivers

The river is faster than a snake slithering for food,
It swirls like a snail in its shell,
It trickles as it ripples, as it goes on all day long,
And it flows like a great white shark.

The water is soft and smooth like a sofa,
The water is a blue crystal,
As clear as a tear.

It ripples and cripples like the salty sea,
And it falls and it calls,
As it goes down into the sea.

Megan Carlin (9)
Elworth Hall Primary School

Rivers

Rivers rush and rivers gush,
Rivers splash and rivers bash,
Rivers flow faster than a cheetah,
Running down the road,
Rivers are faster than a train at full speed,
Rivers smash against the rocks
And bash against the sides.

Richard Coomer (10)
Elworth Hall Primary School

The River

Rivers flow fast,
Like a cheetah,
Trickling and
Rippling, gushing,
Waves, drip-drop
Drip-drop!

Alex Moore (9)
Elworth Hall Primary School

Waterfall

Water crashing onto rocks,
The water is roaring,
It sounds like it is boring,
But it isn't really because the water crashes onto rocks,
It is like small rivers,
And it never ever quivers.

It is an amazement for people staring,
The water sounds like it isn't very caring,
It goes up the sides,
And the water always hides,
Behind the rocks.

Splish-splash, splish-splash,
Water gushing down and around,
Water not making a sound,
It is a monster grabbing out,
The water not making any drought,
The water looks like shining glass.

Sophie Bateman (9)
Elworth Hall Primary School

The Ocean

When I look at the ocean every day,
I see huge stallions galloping across the waves.

When I look at the ocean every day,
I see huge tsunami waves, crashing against the caves.

When I look at the ocean every day,
I see the waves dying down and going back out to sea.

When I walk home every day,
I see some clouds quite full of rain.

When I walk home every day,
I see some puddles like rock pools near the sea.

Martin McLaughlin (9)
Elworth Hall Primary School

Tidal Wave

It charges through the water
Like an irritated bull,
It washes up cities
But it ain't that dull,
It's a raging bull,
Unlikely to stop,
All those people just go plop.

It's creeping up to get you!

Daniel Ashcroft (10)
Elworth Hall Primary School

Waterfall

At the top, ripple, ripple, ripple, then it falls,
After it's fallen you hear a call,
All the water gushing down, then crashing into rocks,
It is so big, it will not fit in a box,
It is quiet like a bird,
Not a sound or a word.

Amy Kay (9)
Elworth Hall Primary School

Waterfalls

Waterfalls are rocks falling from the sky,
As fast as a car at 100 miles an hour,
Falling uncontrollably.

Waterfalls are crystals shimmering in the sun,
Waterfalls are dangerous like lorries spinning around,
Water splashing about.

Shannon Jean Mary West (9)
Elworth Hall Primary School

The Waterfall

It's a big giant shower,
As big as a tower,
You'll feel the cold,
If you're that bold.

It's fast as a stallion,
As it rumbles past,
It's a dragon,
Never coming last.

So as if it knew,
When you were scared,
Roaring louder,
When you're unprepared.

You will be inspired,
From the moment you set sight,
You will know it's massive
From the morning light.

Joseph Watts (9)
Elworth Hall Primary School

Waterfall

The water falls from the sky
Like a pebble from space,
Water hitting the rocks.

The water splashing,
Sloshing, hitting
The bottom like
Giants punching the wall.

The water splashing,
Trickling down to the ocean,
Waterfalls are paradise.

North Green (9)
Elworth Hall Primary School

The Big Waves

The waves are like stallions jumping about,
The waves are like trees waving around,
The waves are crashing against the rocks,
The waves are like giants in blue socks,
The waves are like monsters stomping around everywhere!

Connor Flowers (9)
Elworth Hall Primary School

Streams

The stream is as long as a slithery snake,
Streams are as big as elephants,
Gushing rippling water flowing along,
Waves going along like white horses,
The stream flows as it goes.

Alana Hitchen (9)
Elworth Hall Primary School

Mrs Wright

My very mean teacher, Mrs Wright
Said to us, 'Please don't fight!'
Then she went barmy
And learnt origami
Then fought with all her might!

Megan Johnstone (9)
Kingsley St John's CE Primary School

If

(Based on 'If' by Rudyard Kipling)

If you can keep your cool when everyone
Else is losing their cool
If you can believe in yourself when all people
Tease you
If you can keep your patience and not be tired
Of being patient
Or don't sort things out by using lies
Or if someone hates you don't be horrible back
And don't show off because people
May not like you
And won't want to talk to you.

If you can do things and
Not dream of them
If you can think of great things and realise
They can be done
If you can carry on with
And don't boast about things
If you can bear to hear the truth
That you speak
Or if things you work hard for are broken
Try, try again
And try to cheer people up without lies.

If you can speak your tone and lose your nerve
Or walk with kings but keep your cool
If people don't like you try to get along
If all people count with you but none too many
If you can fill the unforgiving minute
With sixty seconds worth of your life
Yours is the plant
And what more you'll be a person, my friend!

Cammille Doran (10)
Kingsley St John's CE Primary School

The Simpsons

Well where can we start?
The cheekiest in the family is Bart,
He's rubbish in school especially art.

The second is Lisa, she's really small,
But the results in school say it all,
And as a treat, she visits the mall.

Maggie's the one with big teeth,
You stop and wonder if she's a thief,
But then again she'll make a good chief.

Then there's the one with blue hair,
She's had a couple of run-ins for mayor,
But then again she's not a fan of the fair.

Homer's always drinkin' beer,
But he doesn't show much fear
And now and then he fights a deer.

Christopher Stoddart (10)
Kingsley St John's CE Primary School

Digging Dinosaurs

I dug into the Cretaceous period, I might have found a T-rex,
I didn't.
I dug into the Jurassic period, I might have found a brachiosaurus,
I didn't.
I dug into the Triassic period, I might have found a velociraptor,
I didn't.
All I found was an odd-looking stone,
A dinosaur bone!

Luci Glassbrook (9)
Kingsley St John's CE Primary School

If

(Based on 'If' by Rudyard Kipling)

If you can stay calm when others can't,
And are blaming it on you, don't react and blame it on them,
If you can believe you can do it when people doubt you,
But understand their doubting too,
If you can be patient and not be tired of patience
Or if you are being lied about don't lie back,
Or if you are being hated don't hate back,
And don't show off, you won't have any friends.

If you can dream but don't always think they're real,
If you think, don't always make it your aim, you could change
your mind,
If you win don't show off, if you lose don't sulk,
And treat everyone the same,
If you can bear it when you have to tell the truth,
Twisted by fools to make a trap for you,
Or don't react if people break your most precious things,
And try to build them up again, try and try.

If you can talk to people with good words,
Or walk with people and not lose your touch,
If you cannot be hurt by little things,
If you have friends that count on you, don't betray them
If you can forgive people that betray you,
With sixty seconds that keep on going,
Yours is the Earth and everything that is in it,
And which in you'll be a man my son.

George Waring (9)
Kingsley St John's CE Primary School

If

(Based on 'If' by Rudyard Kipling)

If you can hold your nerve when all around you
Are losing theirs, just keep your cool
If you trust yourself even though others don't
But understand their reasons
If you like something so much be patient for it
Or if they're lying about you don't stoop as low
Or someone hates you don't hate them back
And don't boast because you'll find they don't like you.

If you cannot let dreams take over your life
If you cannot think too much about yourself
If you can get on with your life
And treat the weird just the same
If you can say the bad to make it good
Twisted by troublemakers to make a prank
Or you've given everything but it doesn't work
And finish them off with old stuff.

If you can talk to everyone and not brag
Or walk with popularity and still be yourself
If you don't hurt anyone in actions or words
If they all like you, give them trust
If you can make every minute count
With doing everything quite quickly
Yours is the Earth and everything that's in it
And which is more, you'll be a man, my son!

Owen Rowlands (10)
Kingsley St John's CE Primary School

If

(Based on 'If' by Rudyard Kipling)

If you can keep your cool when everyone else
Is losing their cool,
If you can believe in yourself when other people tease you,
But understand why they doubt,
If you can keep your patience and not be teased by being patient,
Or don't sort it out by telling lies,
Of if someone hates don't hate back,
And don't show off because they won't want to talk to you.

If you can dream but don't always think they're real,
If you can think and don't always make your aim,
If you can win and don't show off,
And treat everyone the same,
If you can bear it when you have to tell the truth,
Twisted by fools to make a trap for you,
Or don't react to people who break your most precious things,
And try to fix them up and try to keep confident in yourself.

If you can talk with people and stay good,
Or walk with important people and keep your friends,
If neither enemies nor friends can hurt you,
If everyone counts on you but everyone the same,
If you can fill your spare time because time doesn't wait for you,
With one minute, with hard work,
Yours is the Earth and everyone that's in it,
And which is more, you'll be a man, my son.

Catherine Hunt (9)
Kingsley St John's CE Primary School

If

(Based on 'If' by Rudyard Kipling)

If you can keep your cool when everyone else is losing their cool,
If you can believe in yourself when all people tease you
But understand why they doubt
If you can keep your patience and not be tired of being patient
Or don't sort it out in lies
Or if someone hates, don't be horrible back
And don't show off because people won't want to talk to you.

If you can dream but not think they're real
If you can think of something don't always do it
And not boast if you win or moan if you lose
If you say something that later turns against you
Remember it's your own fault
Don't make deals with dodgy people because they
Will make you look like a fool
And keep trying till you can do it.

If you can talk to hundreds of people at one time
And still be normal
Or be with famous people and not show off
If enemies or friends can't upset you
If everyone is special, don't have one super special friend
If you can keep your life busy and not stop to rest
Yours is the Earth and everything in it
And which is more, you'll be a man, my son.

Jordan Stockdale (9)
Kingsley St John's CE Primary School

If

(Based on 'If' by Rudyard Kipling)

If you can keep your cool when everyone else is losing their cool
If you can believe in yourself when all people tease you
But understand why they doubt you
If you can keep your patience and not be tired of being patient,
Or don't sort it out by using lies
Or if someone hates, don't be horrible back,
And don't show off because people won't want to talk to you,
If you can dream but not let them take over your life
If you can and then do it
If you cannot boast or whinge people will like you
And treat other people the same,
If you can live up to something bad you have said
Twisted by sly people
Or if you want to do something else
And build up the bad people.
If you can talk to crowds and keep your cool
Or walk with famous people and still act normal
If enemies or friends can hurt you
If you all act together but not too powerful
If you can keep busy
With good use of your time
Yours is the Earth and everyone that's in it
And which is more, you'll be a man, my son!

Simon Stubbs (9)
Kingsley St John's CE Primary School

On The Slip Slap Slop

(Based on 'The Ning Nang Nong' by Spike Milligan)

On the Slip Slap Slop
Where the snakes all say blop
And the rabbits love to clean
There's a Slop Slip Slap
Where the bats look like rats
And cats love to wear a bean
On the Slap Slop Slip
All the rats say clip
And you just don't want to look at them
So it's Slip Slap Slop
Snake says blop
Slop Slip Slap
Bats look like rats
Slap Slop Slip
Cats love to wear a bean
What a noisy place to be
It's the Slip Slap Slip Slap Slop!

Danielle Stanley (9)
Kingsley St John's CE Primary School

On The Bing Bang Boo!

(Based on 'The Ning Nang Nong' by Spike Milligan)

On the Bing Bang Boo
When the cats go coo
And the donkeys all say quack
There's a Boo Bang Bing
Where the dogs go ping
And the birds have hurt their back
On the Boo Bing Bang
All the pigs talk slang
And they always hide in a sack
So it's a Bing Bang Boo
Cats go coo
Boo Bang Bing
Dogs go ping
Boo Bing Bang
Pigs talk slang
What a skilful place to belong
It's the Boo Bing Boo Bing Bong!

Sophia Smith & James Faint (9)
Kingsley St John's CE Primary School

Listen To The Rhythm

Come here girl
Listen to the beat
Listen to the rhythm
Of my hip hop feet.

Dancing round the corner
Dancing down the street
Listen to the rhythm
Of my trip trap feet.

Running through the playground
Finding friends to meet
Listen to the rhythm
Of my slip slap feet.

Skipping in the sunshine
Let me feel the heat
Listen to the rhythm
Of my hip hop, slip slap,
Trip trap feet.

Sophie Reynolds (10)
Kingsley St John's CE Primary School

On The Wing Wang Wong

(Based on 'The Ning Nang Nong' by Spike Milligan)

On the Wing Wang Wong
Where the donkeys go long
And the benches all say glue
There is a Wong Wing Wang
Where the gates go clang
And the wheels all say owe
There is a Wong Wang Wing
Where the houses all go ping
And you can't catch them when they do
So it is a Wing Wang Wong
Donkeys go long
Wong Wing Wang
Gates go clang
Wong Wang Wing
Houses all go ping
What a dumb place to belong
On the Wing Wang Wing Wang Wong.

David Holt (10)
Kingsley St John's CE Primary School

Silence

Silence is white like a snowflake,
My eyes see a lonely picture,
My hands stretch out and feel shimmering petals,
The smell is of nothing,
It sounds like I am the only one,
The taste is of nothing,
Silence reminds me of sadness and loneliness.

Jennifer Wiggins (7)
Ladybrook Primary School

Anger And Happiness

Anger is red like a fire-breathing dragon,
Anger tastes like red-hot chillies,
My eyes see a volcano spitting lava,
My hands stretch and feel rocks crushing my fingers,
The smell is like dirty air drifting up my nose,
It sounds like glass crashing on the floor,
Anger reminds me of fighting brothers.

But . . .

Happiness is yellow like a blazing ray of sunshine,
Happiness tastes like candyfloss popping on my tongue,
My eyes see a bird flying in the sky,
My hands stretch out and feel a soft dandelion,
The smell is like daisies drifting up my nose,
It sounds like giggling,
Happiness reminds me of when I ride my bike.

Adam Farrell (7)
Ladybrook Primary School

Anger And Happiness

Anger is red like a fiery volcano,
It sounds like lava crashing down,
Anger tastes like crisps - salty and spicy,
The smell is like hot dogs burning on the barbecue,
Sizzling and furious,
My eyes see me sad and lonely on my bed,
My hands stretch and hug my mum.

Happiness is joyful, children playing out in the blue sparkly sky,
It sounds like birds singing high up in the sky,
Happiness tastes like candyfloss melting in the sun,
The smell is like fresh splish-splashing raindrops falling on my hand,
My eyes see a sparkly moon lighting up the night-time,
My hands stretch out and feel like tickling the rich lightning.

Adam Plant (8)
Ladybrook Primary School

Young Writers - Once Upon A Rhyme Poems From Cheshire

Hate And Happiness

Hate is the grey of a gravestone,
It tastes of blood,
My eyes see the Devil dancing and cackling,
My hands stretch out and feel pain,
It sounds like a scream in the night,
The smell is like emptiness drifting up my nose,
It reminds me of tears.

But . . .

Happiness is pink like the petal of a rose,
It tastes like chocolate,
My eyes see a shining unicorn,
My hands stretch out and feel warmth,
It sounds like the whooshing of birds' wings,
The smell is like the scent of a rose,
It reminds me of the soft coat of a fawn.

Emily Whelan (7)
Ladybrook Primary School

The Giant

The giant screamed
With a monstrous mouth
Like a hole in the ground,
His enormous tummy like
A burger from McDonald's,
His ginormous long legs
Walking wide like
A tall giraffe.
Huge arms waving
About like branches
On a oak tree,
His colossal face as
Powerful as a petrol
Tanker at Tescos.

Alistair Barnes (11)
Ladybrook Primary School

From A Railway Carriage

(Based on 'From A Railway Carriage' by Robert Louis Stevenson)

Quicker than eagles, quicker than rockets,
Buildings and towers, shops and markets,
And speeding along like drivers in races
All through the cities, the cars and buses:
All of the sights of the town and the factories
Oh look, someone's lost their keys
And ever again, in the wink of an eye,
Colourful buildings pass by.

Here is a businessman going to work,
Buying a coffee from Central Perk;
Here is a cat which hides and cowers;
And there is a bird who flies around towers!
Here is a station unfriendly and cold
There is a tramp, lonely and old,
And here is a man and there is Trevor;
Each a glimpse and gone forever!

Ross Wiggins (10) & Jordan Holland (11)
Ladybrook Primary School

Fear

Fear is like a burning fire,
The smell is something burning,
Fear tastes like hot chilli peppers on my tongue,
My eyes see a Devil covered in flames,
My hands stretch out and feel hot metal,
It sounds like madness.

Raqim Mohammed (7)
Ladybrook Primary School

Anger And Happiness

Anger is red like a fiery dragon,
My eyes see an eye with blood pouring down,
My hands stretch out and feel a witch locking me up in a tower,
The smell is like angry breath,
It sounds like a noisy noise,
Anger tastes like a red ball of fire,
Anger reminds me of hot sand burning my feet.

But . . .

Happiness is yellow like a ray of sunshine,
My eyes see a bird up in the sky,
My hands stretch out and feel the lovely clean air,
The smell is like perfume drifting up my nose,
It sounds like birds tweeting in the air,
Happiness tastes like a sweet and sour Harribo on my tongue,
Happiness reminds me of having fun.

Chris Johnson (7)
Ladybrook Primary School

Fear And Love

Fear is like a dark and gloomy, spooky night,
My hands stretch out and feel a demon,
It sounds like groaning,
The smell is like potions and liquids,
My eyes see a roaring lion,
It reminds me of fear,

But . . .

Love is like a sparkling diamond,
My hands stretch out and feel a cuddly, snugly teddy bear,
It sounds like cheerfully singing birds,
The smell is like pink, puffy, sugary candyfloss,
My eyes see a love heart,
Love reminds me of rainbows.

Charlotte Butler (7)
Ladybrook Primary School

Hate And Love

Hate is black, like vampire bats,
My hands stretch out and feel their sharp teeth,
The smell is like blood drifting up my nose,
Hate tastes like demons, bitter on my tongue,
It sounds like thunder,
My eyes see a nightmare,
Hate reminds me of murders.

But . . .

Love is like red hearts,
My hands stretch out and feel my honey bun,
The smell is like sweet perfume drifting up my nose,
Love tastes like candyfloss, sweet on my tongue,
It sounds like birds singing,
My eyes see a beautiful thing,
Love reminds me of happiness.

Alexander Beecroft (7)
Ladybrook Primary School

Laughter

Laughter is silver like a bright night star in the sky,
The smell is like fresh summer breezes in the air,
Laughter tastes like nothing,
My eyes see a bunch of children happy and joyful,
It sounds like the cheerful kids running about,
My hands stretch out and feel cold, winter snow,
Laughter reminds me of Christmas fun.

Kieran Kenny (8)
Ladybrook Primary School

Young Writers - Once Upon A Rhyme Poems From Cheshire

From A Railway Carriage

(Based on 'From A Railway Carriage' by Robert Louis Stevenson)

Faster than aeroplanes, faster than cars,
Bridges and stadium, pavements and bars,
And racing along, just like Formula 1,
All through the city, faster than a marathon:
All of the sights of football fans in boots
Seeing men in fancy suits;
And ever again in the wink of an eye,
Hearing babies about to cry.

Here is a canine barking with fury,
Passing McDonald's and a lorry;
Here is a cat that is miaowing;
And there is a little child who is screaming.
Here is a fly as fast as a bird,
Here is a man reading a word
And here is a bike and there is Trevor
Each a glimpse and gone forever!

Daniel Price (11)
Ladybrook Primary School

From A Railway Carriage

(Based on 'From A Railway Carriage' by Robert Louis Stevenson)

Quicker than jet planes, quicker than a mouse,
Restaurants and cafés, a building and a house,
And sliding along like snakes in some tall grass,
All through the city the shops that we pass:
All the sights of taxis and buses
Each a blur as it passes,
And ever again in the wink of an eye,
Heald Green station whizzes by.

Jack Griffiths (10)
Ladybrook Primary School

From A Railway Carriage

(Based on 'From A Railway Carriage' by Robert Louis Stevenson)

Faster than Concorde, faster than Porsches,
Towns and city centres, pubs and offices,
And brave firemen sprinting to huge fires,
All through the pollution, cars and lorries:
All the sights of the road and bridges
Birds perch on tower ledges;
And ever again in the wink of an eye,
Huge football grounds whistle by.

Here is a woman filled with tension,
All by herself collecting her pension,
Here is a man going to work,
And there is a big man who stands and smirks,
Here is a car coming out of a drive,
Here are some planes taking a dive
And here is a truck, and here is a car,
Each a glimpse and gone forever!

Christopher Taylor & Luke Cartwright (10)
Ladybrook Primary School

A Modern Version Of 'From A Railway Carriage'
(Based on the poem by Robert Louis Stevenson)

Quicker than a racehorse, quicker than jet planes,
Factories and cafés, buildings and trains,
And sliding along like a cobra in grass
All through the city the shops that we pass
All of the sights of the trams and children
Rush by in the city sun;
And ever again in the wink of an eye,
Lines of houses race nearby.

Here is a man who is running away,
Runs from the shop because he has not paid;
Here is a child left all on his own;
And there is a dog who has stolen a bone!
Here is a bridge with cars driving over
Murky waters of the river;
And here is a boat, and there is a docker:
Each a glimpse and gone forever!

Fiona Farnsworth (10)
Ladybrook Primary School

A Modern Version of 'From A Railway Carriage'

(Based on the poem by Robert Louis Stevenson)

Quicker than Concorde, quicker than lorries,
Pylons and tunnels, bridges and quarries,
And rushing along like horses in races,
All through the city, shops and lorry bases:
All of the sights of the cars and the shops
Zoom past like speeding cops;
And ever again, in the wink of an eye,
Towers of grey flats fly by.

Here is a factory pumping thick, black smoke,
Over the city, making people choke;
Here is a woman looking at the shops,
And there is a child who likes looking at tops!
Here is a car broken down in the road
Carrying an enormous load;
And here is a school, and there is grey weather:
Each a glimpse and gone forever!

Gemma Clarke & Sally Hind (10)
Ladybrook Primary School

A Modern Version Of 'From A Railway Carriage'

(Based on 'From A Railway Carriage' by Robert Louis Stevenson)

Quicker than lightning, louder than thunder,
Dodging and hiding, over and under
And racing along like a red Ferrari,
All through the night, polluted sky is starry:
All of the sights of the graveyards and trees
We pass as fast as the bees;
And ever again in the wink of an eye,
The spirits rise, bodies die.

Here is a city with lights on and off,
Here are the factories making people cough;
Here is a farm with cattle in the fields;
And there is a museum showing shields!
Here is a park where all the children play
Laughing and singing every day;
And there is the rain, and there is bad weather:
Each a glimpse and gone forever!

Ella Callaghan Rhodes & Juliet Booth (10)
Ladybrook Primary School

From A Railway Carriage

(Based on 'From A Railway Carriage' by Robert Louis Stevenson)

Quicker than cheetahs, quicker than planes,
Sports cars and buildings, factories and trains,
And zooming along past the city and cops,
All through the city, buildings and shops:
All the sights of urbanisation
Zoom by amidst collisions
And ever again, in the wink of an eye,
Cold metal stations fly by.

Here is a puff of smoke from a man's pipe,
Going into the shop to buy some tripe;
Here is a child who watches and waits;
And there is a town square for meeting your mates!
Here is a truck delivering its load
Speeding right down the road;
And here is the street, and there is a river:
Each a glimpse and gone forever!

Jack Gilmartin & Alun Davies (10)
Ladybrook Primary School

From A Railway Carriage

(Based on 'From A Railway Carriage' by Robert Louis Stevenson)

Quicker than lightning, quicker than tr-ams,
Tourists and statues, children and pr-ams,
And speeding down the track like dogs chasing some cats,
All through the city, people wearing cool hats;
All of the sights of the shops and lorries
Kids outside, licking lollies;
And ever again, in the wink of an eye,
Shops and houses pass by.

Here is a skyscraper up in the sky,
Children are waving as we pass them by;
Here is a shop full of toys
And here is a school full of young boys!
Here is a lady dressed all in yellow
And those girls fancy that fellow;
And here is the rain, and there is bad weather:
Each a glimpse and gone forever!

Emma Tyler & Daniela Taylor (10)
Ladybrook Primary School

My Special Poem

Happy as a happy memory,
Loving people care for you,
People giving hope and joy,
People buying brand new toys.

Holly Devereux (10)
Lostock Hall Primary School

The Season

The sun is shining in the sky
Just as the moon waves goodbye
It is hot but the moon is not
As the birds are flying by.
The kids are lying about the time
It is 2 o'clock in the morning
Now it is really pouring
The leaves are falling from the sky
So mums are making lots of pies
The birds are starting to go south
Kids are saying, 'Put mince pie in my mouth.'
Going to bed on Christmas Eve's really cool
No one is eating gruel
The snow is now falling
Cancelled sporting
The creatures are all inside
I am turning to ice, oh my!
So now it's spring
But don't go without a ping
All the animals are born
No clothing is torn
The sun is twinkling in the sky so big
But I won't have a better year with seasons like this.

Shelley Owen (10)
Lostock Hall Primary School

One By One

One by one
one by one
I am dancing
in the sun.

Two by two
two by two
I am playing
at the zoo.

Three by three
three by three
I am playing
in a tree.

Four by four
four by four
I like playing
on the floor

Five by five
five by five
I am going
out for a drive.

Six by six
six by six
I like playing
with sticks.

Seven by seven
seven by seven
I like playing
up in Heaven.

Eight by eight
eight by eight
I am climbing
over a gate.

Nine by nine
nine by nine
I am
fine.

Ten by ten
ten by ten
I have seen
a hen.

Emily Brennan (6)
Lostock Hall Primary School

The Teacher Who Lived In A School

There once was a teacher who lived in a school,
She taught us to write as a rule.
We sat in front of the board each day,
But what did she do when we were out at play?
She went to the cupboard and got some books,
If they had fallen off, she put coats on hooks.
She needed a pillow for under her head,
But she used maths books for a pillow instead.
She used paper for a cover,
One sheet, two sheets and another,
Bell rings, whistle blows,
Stand still, don't blow your nose.
Line up in single file,
Line up in an orderly style.
Doors open, bell rings,
Go inside, do lots of things.
Bell rings again, go home,
Where is the teacher? Nobody knows,
Oh teacher, where could she be?
Hope she's not in bed with me!

Charlotte Brennan (10)
Lostock Hall Primary School

A Poem About Spring

Springtime has come
the birds hum
will they stop
or will they pop?

Night-time is silent
and nobody is violent
the birds have gone to bed
and not a word is said.

The phone has rung
morning has sprung
people lie in bed
not matter what is said.

The evening has come
it will not spoil your fun
lay your head down
without a frown.

Leah Ward (10)
Lostock Hall Primary School

Horse Riding

I love horse riding, I love it so much
I go to Bank Farm Riding School.
It puts a smile on my face.
My lessons are done, let's have a race.
There are lots of horses that I ride.
One of them was four feet wide.
He was ginger, with a bucket on his face.
Now it's time for another race.
I go horse riding at 9am on Saturday,
Then on Sunday I'm out all day.
Now I can't have a rest, it's Monday.
Oh no, it's a schoolday!

Katie Trollope (10)
Lostock Hall Primary School

Pet Care

Play with the dog,
Chasing the frog.
Feed the fish,
In the dish.
Cat in the house,
Chasing a mouse.
Rabbit in the garden,
Chewing on a carrot.
Hamster in the running wheel,
I love the way it squeals.
Rats in a cage
Which looks like a cave.
Snake on my bed,
Looking around with its tiny head.
Horse in a stable,
Eating his dinner on a table.
Bird eating berries up a tree,
Here comes a cat
Who nearly grabs his knee.

Mia Lees (8)
Lostock Hall Primary School

A Fast Sniper

A sniper is an eagle
Soaring through the sky,
Looking down on its prey,
Waiting with no sound at all.

Aiming with one beady eye,
It catches a mouse down by.
Putting it between its claws
And now its victim lives - no more.

Michael James Thompson (9)
Manor House Primary School

The Snow Spider

The winter seems like a long-legged spider,
Weaving her web of sadness,
She shows no mercy to her helpless victims,
She covers the land with a sticky film,
No one dares withstand it.

Something has disturbed the snow spider,
Something has made her worry,
As the bright sun rises overhead,
She begins to slowly melt,
The snow spider is going.

So until next time the web has fallen,
The people may relax and be warm,
But the snow spider will be back again,
Oh yes, she will be back,
So for now it's farewell from the snow spider,
And the future is rather black.

Oliver Thompson (10)
Manor House Primary School

The Wise Old Owl

I am an old owl stuck in a tree,
counting people, one, two, three.
Sleep all day,
play all night.
Playing with conkers
makes me bonkers.
I see the sun rise
so I go back to sleep.
Then autumn comes,
then I hibernate for a week!

Tassha Jones (9)
Manor House Primary School

Winter

Winter is a mighty bear,
Giant and fierce,
Lying in his lair
Waiting . . . waiting.

Out he comes,
Ground freezes,
Cold wind,
The water turns to ice.

Along he bounds,
Shaggy fur,
Sharp claws,
A ferocious killer.

Snow melting,
Plants sprouting,
Bear weakening,
Spring again!

Hazel Clarke (10)
Manor House Primary School

The Nest Egg

There once was a woman called Ann
Who had a precious hen.
It laid a golden egg,

He! He! Ho! Ho! She thought,
If I feed it twice as much
It will lay me twice as many.
Oh deary Henny-penny!

And one day her greediness was so bad
She gave it far too much till it overloaded.
The fed-up hen exploded.

Alex Jones (9)
Manor House Primary School

The Tornado

The tornado is a raging dinosaur,
Very grey indeed,
Waiting to gobble up whatever comes before it.
Its mighty tongue helps as it swallows everything whole.

His great, whetted teeth grab his weary prey
He's mighty vicious and raging,
Destructive in every way
And his angry mood's not changing.

He swiftly gallops to the next town
And makes them pray for life.
Which way next, up or down?
His massive claws, like a bloody knife.

Jade Ireland (11)
Manor House Primary School

Thunder And Lightning

Thunder and lightning is a ferocious lion,
Dangerous and mighty,
Quickly he moves across the land,
Across the sea and over the sand.

Loudly he roars to frighten his prey,
Raging like mad all night and all day,
And when night comes he settles down,
So quiet, so calm he lies on the ground.

Through the night he sleeps without a sound,
Now he can never, ever be found,
Until he comes out to hunt again,
His prey will no longer suffer any pain.

Matthew Furlong (10)
Manor House Primary School

The Raging Fire

The raging fire is your wild parents,
Angry and fierce.
One warm and gentle,
The other, the burning, blazing mass
At the top of the pack.

She's always warm and loving,
Colourful and bright.
Mood changing from day to night,
It can be a comforting delight.

As he spits his fiery flames
For people pray for him to change,
Moving and inspiring as it may be.

Erin Sykes (11)
Manor House Primary School

The River

The river is a slippery otter,
Streamlined and swift;
Flowing downstream;
Following the banks.

Speeding up in the current;
He dives down onto the fishes;
Engulfing them silently,
He slips away.

On calm sunny days he slowly slides;
Leisurely swimming along the river bed,
Inconspicuously present;
He waits.

Nic Simpkin (10)
Manor House Primary School

Aeroplane

Aeroplane is a fierce dragon
A noisy, fiery danger;
Flying through the sky,
Evil, giant and hungry.

If he sees you standing
He'll swoop down and kill you.
So if you see him coming
Run or else he will do.

Matthew Steele (11)
Manor House Primary School

F1 Car

The F1 car is a fierce cheetah,
Spotty and bright,
Speeding wildly through the track,
His strong tail waiting to hit you.

His almighty roar echoes in the ground,
He speeds violently all around,
He swings into gear and speeds towards the horizon
He chases you and then kills you.

Matthew Dawson (10)
Manor House Primary School

Kittens

My two kittens are called Thomas and Tilly
They play all day and are often silly.
They sleep all night, curled up tight
Under the soft moonlight.
In the morning when it is nice and bright.
The kittens come down and start to fight.

Lauren Oultram (10)
Manor House Primary School

A Fierce Volcano

The volcano is a raging dragon
Grey and rough
Still and calm
Waiting . . .

Out he comes
Spotting his prey
They're coming to his lair
He's ready to kill.

There's a rumbling sound
Out he comes
Spilling his lava
Killing his prey.

Jamie London (10)
Manor House Primary School

The Volcano

The volcano is a fierce dragon,
Destructive and powerful,
He roars above all sound,
Waiting and rumbling.

And then he opens his beady eyes,
And scans across the ground,
Suddenly he makes an almighty attack,
And breathes fire round and round.

He suddenly turns into a killing machine,
And destroys anything he sees,
He is a powerful rampage moving quickly,
Leaving nothing alive behind.

Adam Reeves (11)
Manor House Primary School

The Terrifying Tornado

The tornado is a roaring 'mum'
Praying for the wind,
Holding on for the night,
Waiting to spring.

The wind, so tight,
Ready to fight,
Speeding across the ground,
A mighty roar all around.

The air stills,
The world crams,
It stops the kills,
Waiting to strike again.

Mark Heighton (10)
Manor House Primary School

A Bed

A bed is a squishy octopus,
Colourful and bright
Luring his prey in . . .
For the night.

He constricts his victims
With his sheets,
Gradually getting tighter
While they sleep.

All through the night
He holds on tight
With all his might
Until the light breaks through.

Tom Halliwell (11)
Manor House Primary School

Volcano

The volcano is a killer bear,
Brown and fierce.
Dormant, waiting to have its lunch
It spots its prey on the ground.

It is not dormant any more,
It's active now.
The bear has spotted its prey,
It's chasing its prey.

It has caught its prey,
It's had its prey for lunch.
The village is a burning mass.
Then it eats you for lunch with an almighty
. . . *Crunch, crunch, crunch.*

Philip Sparke (10)
Manor House Primary School

The Bed

The bed is like a lazy cat,
Cuddly and cosy.
He is lying there, waiting
For me to come along.

He is ready to be worn out,
Like a shriek machine.
But that's not the bed I know,
Dead, bad and mean.

I run to stop it changing,
Into someone else.
I stop it just in time,
Now it is its quiet, sleepy self.

Thomas Stockton (10)
Manor House Primary School

My Puppy

Juno is a Bouvier
She jumps up and down
She rather reminds me
Of a clown.

She runs around
And flops about
She brings her toys
And takes them out.

She runs under the table
And wrecks the house
Up the stairs
And round about.

She barks and barks
At all who pass
Until we take her
In to task.

And that's my puppy
A naughty girl
But to me she is
The best in the world.

George McCormick (8)
Manor House Primary School

The Clashing Waterfall

A waterfall is a fierce and beautiful golden eagle
Ruling the sky.
It shrieks as it dives for its prey with great force
It is known as an extreme killing machine.

His noise echoes around as he brings
His victims to the ground
With his great sound.

Michael Nield (10)
Manor House Primary School

The Winter

The winter is a white snow wolf,
As fast as the lightning can go,
As white as the snow itself,
But is as deadly as the foe.

The winter sounds like thunder,
But so does a wolf's stomach,
Ready to eat
And ready to go,
As the sun comes.

The snow wolf has done his work,
And it is time to leave and go
From the sun through the summer,
Hibernating as they sleep and rest,
And ready to go again.

Connor Karl Bladen (10)
Manor House Primary School

Planets

Planets are bouncy balls bounced high into the sky
They are baseballs hit up into the night.
Planets are light bulbs shining on the earth
They are flowers hanging from Heaven.
Planets are balloons that float up and never come down.
They are snowballs thrown at the clouds
Planets are coconuts thrown up into dark space
They are giant eggs painted in all different colours
That were laid by a giant chicken.
That's planets!

Dominic Howard (9)
Manor House Primary School

Firework!

A bird is a zooming firework
Firework, higher than the sky
It is as colourful as a parrot,
It flies like a rocket
At 100 miles per hour
It reflects off the sun,
It screeches like a firework
Touching the clouds.

It is colourful and bright,
It can pop in the air
When it is angry
It flies high in the sky
You can just about see it
Swerve up in the sky.

Daniel Mulhern (11)
Manor House Primary School

The Volcano

A volcano is a cat; a raging ball of fur.
All red and white.
Sleeping; then explodes with the speed of a bullet.
All hot and spiky, hungry for disaster.

Destroying cupboards, carpets, couches, county and country
While speeding over the landscape,
Hurting people and going fiery in no time at all.

But at times he calms down and sleeps all day,
And rests at night curling up in his bed
And goes to sleep for hundreds of years.

Callum Howard (10)
Manor House Primary School

The Chainsaw

The chainsaw is a roaring jaguar
Fast and sharp.
With its razor jagged jaws
Ready to cut up people.

It waits for its prey,
Then clanks into action,
With a grating noise,
It cuts people up.

Josh Slater (10)
Manor House Primary School

Rabbit

I once saw a rabbit jumping and twirling around,
Leaping and running and sliding all at once.
It was a jet-black rabbit that I saw acting mad,
All wriggling and swooshing about.
But where did it come from, this cheeky little monster?
Now that I am not sure,
But one thing I am certain about this crazy little fella
Is he is cuter than a jackdaw.

Jennifer Owens (8)
Manor House Primary School

The Sunrise

The sunrise is the light to my eyes
The sunrise is the brightness in the mid-morning skies
The sunrise is the nicest thing
The sunrise makes the birds sing
The sunrise.

Lauren Yarwood (9)
Manor House Primary School

Flowers

Sunflowers look at the sun
all day long, they have so much fun.
Flowers sway in the breeze
they look like they're dancing.
Roses are colourful
as the nicest shade of red.
Flowers are beautiful colours
like red, blue, white, purple and yellow.
Violets are cool
as the nicest shade of blue from the sea.
Daisies are as white
as a cloud.
Pink carnations are my nan's
favourite flowers.
Poppies are the
colour of the shade of red.
Fuschias are the colour of
the nicest purple you could ever get.
Dandelions are a funny flower,
they are the colour of the desert sand.

Steven Moores (9)
Manor House Primary School

My Nana

My nana is a smooth, shimmery petal
A golden tulip always open for me
A silver star gleaming at me
A soft teddy bear cuddling me
She is the angel at the top of my Christmas tree
She is a leaf softly dancing in the wind with me
She is a blanket wrapping around me night and day
That's my nana.

Georgia Merry (9)
Manor House Primary School

World War II

It looks like an elephant has trodden on the buildings!
It's a horrible sight.
It's like someone has glued your mouth together.
You've got so many things running through your mind.
Questions, so many questions.
But in a way you're lucky but you don't know why.
You're so confused.
You don't know where to go, what to do
It's like you're glued to the spot
You're scared, so scared.
You wish the bombs would stop.
But you do want the bombs to fall
Because if they fall now it will be over and done with.
You wish that with one word it would stop.
No!

Katherine Sparke (8)
Manor House Primary School

Thank You For The Senses

Thank you for the morning light,
Thank you for the flowers in sight.

What we see and hear is good.

Thank you for my friends I found,
Thank you for the family around.

What we smell and feel is great.

Thank you for how we play and feel,
Thank you for what is beautiful and real.

What we know and own is life,
What we have is love and strife.

Lauren Riddoch (10)
Manor House Primary School

My Cat Poppy

My cat Poppy is lazy,
She's like a table on its last legs.
Her fur is like a fluffy cushion.
She has ogre green eyes.
When she has her mad half an hour
She's like a cheetah
Running through the streets of India.
She eats like a tiger cub munching its food
That her mum has just brought back for her.
Her tummy's as big as an elephant.
Her snoring wakes you up
Like a horn sounding in your ear.
When she's ill the clouds blacken
And the rain pours down from the winter sky.
When she is happy the sun comes out
And the flowers grow.

Lucy Ryder (9)
Manor House Primary School

My Nan

My nan is a cuddly koala,
She's a laughing hyena, roaring out loud,
She's a pretty princess.
Her eyes are like the midday sun,
Her lips are as red as rubies.

My nan is a soft petal,
Colourful and bright,
She's a shining star, falling from Heaven,
She's fast asleep when the clock strikes eleven.
When the sun rises, she's awake again,
Laughing and playing, all over again.

Lauren Furlong (9)
Manor House Primary School

My Nan

My nan is a computer,
She's a model.
She's a quiet mouse.
My nan is a rose on a hot summer's day.
My nan is a slow centipede,
She's Jamie Oliver.
She's a cheetah when shopping.
My nan is a chatterbox, because
She never stops chatting.

Lucy Mollat (9)
Manor House Primary School

Going To The Zoo

I go to the zoo
To see the animals
To see the kangaroo
And the lions and the tigers.

Cheetahs and jaguars climb the trees
Monkeys swing and make lots of noise
We always watch the chimpanzees
Then we go to the shop and buy some toys.

David Thompson (7)
Manor House Primary School

Snake

It moves like a ballerina,
going through the sharp grass.
Its body shimmers in the sun,
it brings light into the world.
It never speaks, its body just saying,
it's coming, it's coming to get you.

Samantha Morgan (9)
Manor House Primary School

Scary Poem

I live in a house
I see a woodlouse!
Burnt pancakes
Frozen-up lakes.

Curdling screams
Horrible dreams!
What else can I do?
I see oozing goo.

I live with the Adams family
Why are they so deadly?
I hate spiders
The family drinks lots of cider.

I live with the Adams family! *Boo!*

Cecilia Vinchenzo (9)
Manor House Primary School

The Rainforest

Birds beep
Gazelles leap
Leopards pounce
Monkeys bounce
Gorillas stomp
Lions chomp
Snakes glide
Insects fly
Some with jaws
Some with tails
Some with feathers
Some with scales.

Alice Harmer (10)
Manor House Primary School

Animals Under the Sea

I see a dolphin
Jumping through the waves
Racing with its fellow dolphins.
Next a shark comes
The dolphins work as a team
They force the shark to retreat
And the dolphins are shark-free for now.
I see a dolphin, lord of the seas.

I see a shark
Showing off his teeth at the sharks around him
Fighting over a fish
The fight now gets fiercer
Each shark does its best to win the fight
But none will give in
They all want the fish.
I see a shark, king of the killers.

I see a clownfish
Swimming through the reef
Making the water ripple
It is just so little
It's talking to its mates
Having a happy time
With no troubles about it.
I see a clownfish, captain of the jokers.

Madeleine Clarke (8)
Manor House Primary School

Clowns

Clowns are funny and they have lots of money,
They dance all night and prance.
They bounce all night long, to the beat.
They come to parties,
Funny clowns.

Sophie Slater (10)
Manor House Primary School

Cats Can

Cats can bounce
Cats can pounce
Cats can purr or
Lick their fur.

Cats have claws
On their paws
Claws are used for climbing trees
Paws are used for buzzing bees.

Pippa Webber (7)
Manor House Primary School

My Koala

It has fluffy brown fur
And its claws are long, but not sharp.
Its eyes are like fudge,
It can hardly budge.
But then as if by magic
It zooms across the ground for it has heard a noise.
Hunters are coming, but it will hide in a tree and be safe,
So remember if you see one
Remember to say, 'I'm not a hunter!'

Laura-Jane Garvie (9)
Manor House Primary School

Black

Black is the night sky,
A beautiful, black Arab running wild and free,
The stripes on a tiger,
A pair of socks hanging on the line,
Or a fox's ears to listen with,
Maybe a black Labrador running in a field,
Black is a sign of sadness.

Zoe Isles (9)
St Lewis' Primary School, Warrington

The Wonders Of Nature

Green, wooden trees waving
Muddy, watery pond paddling
Waving, green leaves blowing

Poison, swishy berries picking
Wet, crunchy grass gasping
Dirty, brown mud swishing
Colourful, hard stone scattering
Perfect, yellow buttercups singing
Brown, wooden fence sawing
Hard, wooden sticks cracking
Green, crispy weeds cropping
Green, naughty nettles stinging.

Kathryn Gleave
St Lewis' Primary School, Warrington

Where Nature Lies

Water, deep pond paddling
Green brown leaves jumping
Long, mucky grass growing
Red, big berries eating
Black, dirty mud munching
Hard grey stones sleeping
Pretty, lovely flowers dancing
Wooden, wide fence shaking
Thick sticks stunning
Patterns sticking out, weeds walking
Sharp green nettles stinging
Wooden tall trees talking.

Charlotte Woodall (9)
St Lewis' Primary School, Warrington

Red

Red is the colour of a shiny ruby glowing in the dark,
Dripping blood on my hand,
Pouring lava out of an erupting volcano,
Juicy apple lying on the floor,
Cherries hanging on a branch,
Fields covered in poppies,
Flames on a burning building,
Man United shirts coming out of the tunnel,
Red is the colour of Mars.

Aidan Nolan (9)
St Lewis' Primary School, Warrington

White

Seagulls flying in the air,
Swans swimming in the stream,
Snow falling from the sky,
Letters being opened by excited children,
Clouds blocking the sun from shining on beaches,
My favourite white top sitting on the washing line,
Teachers writing on the whiteboards,
Dads going to work in their white shirts,
White is the colour of Christmas.

Olivia Quinn
St Lewis' Primary School, Warrington

Red

Red is the blood dripping from your mouth
The juicy strawberry from the farm
The round planet of Mars floating in the universe
Strawberry milkshake from McDonald's swirling in the cup
The red roses dancing in the mist
The gleaming campfire in the night
Red is the colour of sunset late at night.

James Gleave
St Lewis' Primary School, Warrington

Outdoor World

Wooden, brown log cabin burning,
Spiky green leaves flying,
Long, big trees swaying,
Muddy, wet pond moving,
Thin rectangular gate opening,
Brown wooden fence rattling,
Dark, comfy bench waiting,
Green, round dome dreaming,
Long, thin branch waving,
Rosy-red berries blowing.

Jessica Gorton
St Lewis' Primary School, Warrington

The Nature Trail

Trailing, entrancing trees talking
Perfect, pretty ponds plotting
Rough, lush logs laughing
Flirting, furious fences fuming
Short wood platform performing
Big, dark dome daydreaming
Tall, mucky mound moaning
Rolling, sleeping stones smiling
White, great goalposts gasping
Brown, dirty ditch dancing.

Lydia Smith (9)
St Lewis' Primary School, Warrington

Purple

Purple is a gorgeous Dairy Milk bar wrapper,
The sixth colour in the rainbow,
A pretty petal on a flower,
A purple cloud at dusk,
A purple planet waiting to be discovered,
A purple piece of velvet, soft and silky too,
The perfect purple feathers on a bird,
And a purple feather on a feather boa,
Or a purple pitcher waiting to be looked at,
The purple grapes on a tree,
Purple is the colour of the rainbow.

Eleanor Vize (9)
St Lewis' Primary School, Warrington

Blue

Blue is one of the colours in the Union Jack.
Sea waves crashing into surfers.
Great white sharks biting into whale blubber.
Blue can be the background of a computer.
Dolphins leaping in and out of the sea.
Blue sky can change into grey.
Blue is one of the colours of the rainbow.
Blue is the colour of someone's eyes.
Blue can be a display wallpaper.
Blue can be hair dye for drunken rockers.

Joseph Makin
St Lewis' Primary School, Warrington

Our Nature Trail!

Thick, tall trees waving
Big, juicy berries blinking
Still, straight fences standing
Long, light leaves laughing
Dripping, round raindrops rolling
Blowing, bending bluebells bowing
Still, strong stones starving
Pretty, pink petals playing
Mucky, mushy mud moving
Green, growing grass grazing.

Heather Morgan (9)
St Lewis' Primary School, Warrington

The Nature Trail!

Long, green grass cutting
Wooden, brown fence sitting
Tall, large trees waving
Small, colourful flowers dancing
Red, big berry eating
Blue, clear pond swimming
Wet, muddy steps standing
White, hard goalpost gagging.

Shaun Irving (9)
St Lewis' Primary School, Warrington

Blue

Blue is for water
Blue sky from above
Blue cars dashing by on a motorway
Blue ink on a piece of paper
Blue icicles hanging off the window
Blue jeans covering your legs
Blue animals, like sharks and whales
Blue waves crashing on the rocks
Blue sapphires shining on the ground
Blue is the colour of ice and water.

Lewis Alder (9)
St Lewis' Primary School, Warrington

Nature

Trailing, terrific trees talking,
Perfect, pretty pond paddling,
Flirting, furious fence fishing,
Gulping, green goalposts gasping,
Big, bursting bird box blushing,
Drinking, dirty ditch demanding,
Liking, living log loving,
Driving, daydreaming dome dancing,
Plant, poet platform playing,
Snoring, smiling stepping stones sleeping.

April Rice (9)
St Lewis' Primary School, Warrington

Really Red

The flames of dancing fire of the night
Or the hot, burning lava exploding from a volcano
A bright red apple dropping from a tree
Or the red sky at dusk
Red might be the colour of a planet
Or a plateful of strawberries
The colour of a rose in your garden
Or the colour of strawberry ice cream and milkshake
Or a fire just being lit.

Emma Sherwood
St Lewis' Primary School, Warrington

Orange Is The Light Of The Way

A juicy orange dribbling down my chin.
The sun setting, all big and round
The autumn leaves falling off the tree.
My orange jumper blowing gently in the wind.
A fox running to hide away.
Orange is the colour in the rainbow.
The orange of a gerbera standing in the sun.
Bright orange fireworks in the dark, black sky.
The pretty orange of a robin's breast.

Sean Booth (10) & Sarah Hodgkiss (9)
St Lewis' Primary School, Warrington

Nature, Nature!

Brown wood roots gasping
Orange, pretty leaves dancing
Squeaky, watery mud playing
Sweet, red berries jumping
Brown, sharp branches banging
Round, soft pebbles rolling
Big, colourful tree waving
Blue see-through pond splashing
Yellow, orange daffodils daydreaming
Hard, rough trunk thinking
Muddy, fat wood cracking
Nut-round acorn thumping.

Gabriella Booth
St Lewis' Primary School, Warrington

Our Nature Trail

Thin, wet gasping grass
Hard, brown standing wood
Yellow, hard wailing fence
Shiny, red bouncing berry
Long, big sitting tree
Spiky, green waving bush
Blue, rough washing pond
Evil, naughty plotting plant.

Curtis Giles (9)
St Lewis' Primary School, Warrington

The Colour Blue

Blue is the sky
Or the pool water splashing,
Splashing over the edge,
A blue sports car zooming
Or the colour of part of the rainbow.
Blue is the colour of a bluebell growing
On a summer's day
Or a nice juicy blueberry,
The sea coming in shore on a lovely day.
Blue is the colour of *happiness!*

Sophie Pigg (9)
St Lewis' Primary School, Warrington

Outside Our School!

Gigantic, glistening goalposts gazing
Boring, brown bench sitting
Dirty, smelly bin drooping
Magnificent, muddy mound munching
Old rocky tree waving
Red fireman's rope ladder rocking
Slippy, grey stones sliding
Green, long grass squelching
Painted, colourful wall shining
Blue, round netball goal nursing
Red school gate swinging.

Caitlin Beck (9)
St Lewis' Primary School, Warrington

The Nature Trail

Mucky, wet pond swimming
Wooden, long bench sitting
Green, brown leaves waving
Green, slimy grass sliding
Prickly, tall bush growing
Tall, wide dome dancing
Short, small log sitting
Long, wooden fence standing
High, fat trees talking
Tiny, thin flowers playing.

Courtney Saunders (9)
St Lewis' Primary School, Warrington

The Nature Around You!

Thick, tall trees waving
Big, juicy berries blinking
Straight, still fence standing
Long, light leaves laughing
Round, silky raindrops rolling
Drooping, bending bluebells blowing
Still, strong stones sliding
Pretty pink petals playing
Mucky, mushy mud moving
Green, growing grass grazing.

Stephanie Barrett (10)
St Lewis' Primary School, Warrington

Hedgehogs

What I hate about hedgehogs is
when you put your hand on their backs
they prick you.

What I like about hedgehogs is
when you see their faces.

What I hate about hedgehogs is
when they crawl away into the bushes
and when you can't find them.

What I like about hedgehogs is
when they have their spikes down.

Liam Murphy (7)
St Vincent's RC Junior School, Altrincham

My Brother

What I hate about my brother
is he is always showing off when a friend comes round.
What I like about my brother
is he plays with me on ice hockey.
What I hate about my brother
is he always fights me and when I say stop he carries on
and it hurts a lot.
What I like about my brother
is how he plays racing games on windy and sunny days.

Lili Walker (7)
St Vincent's RC Junior School, Altrincham

Kangaroo!

I am a bouncing kangaroo
I bounce day and night
and always go out of sight.
It is fun to bounce
because you can go anywhere
and never get told off.
My mum shouts me back
so I have to go back
and that's not the end
of my song!
I bounce so fast
you can't catch me.
You see that fire
you can't catch me!

Chloe O'Kell (9)
St Vincent's RC Junior School, Altrincham

Specks Of Dust

Specks of dust
fly in the sky.
Specks of dust
end up in your eye.

Specks of dust
make you sneeze
Specks of dust
make you wheeze.

Specks of dust
are on the ground
Specks of dust are all around.

William Protheroe (9)
St Vincent's RC Junior School, Altrincham

Crabs

What I hate about crabs is
they nip you and click at you
and are horrible to you.

What I like about crabs is
they follow you around.

What I hate about crabs is
they make you bleed and bite you
and dig holes in the sand.

What I like about crabs is
how they walk sideways
and not forwards.

Isobelle Watson (7)
St Vincent's RC Junior School, Altrincham

Battle Boys

What I hate about my cousin James
is how he's such a telltale.

What I like about my cousin James
is how easy it is to scare him.

What I hate about my cousin James
is how annoying he is and how smart he is.

What I like about my cousin James
is he'll play real fun games with me
and how easy it is to beat him at cards.

Daniel Kington (7)
St Vincent's RC Junior School, Altrincham

Rhyme

Once upon a time
I wrote a little rhyme
and here's how it goes . . .
hope you've got the time
It's really very fine
and doesn't cost a dime!

I always have the time
to mime while I rhyme
though it's almost nine!
School starts at nine
so I'm ending my rhyme,
but there is always time to rhyme
another day!

Luke Stewart (8)
St Vincent's RC Junior School, Altrincham

The Things About My Sister

What I hate about my sister is
when she screams down my ear.

What I like about my sister is
when she gives me a great big hug.

What I hate about my sister is
when she takes my teddy off my bed
and tries to hide it.

What I like about my sister
is how she shares her sweets with me.

Francesca Law (8)
St Vincent's RC Junior School, Altrincham

Toffee

What I hate about toffee is that
when you eat it, it is very sticky
and it sticks to your teeth.
What I like about toffee is that
when you put one in your mouth
and bite into it all the sweet taste bursts out
and you just have to have another one.
What I hate about toffee is that
my little brother always wants my last one
and my mum will tell me off if I do not give it to him.
What I like about toffee is
how it gives you that feeling that
when you have to save them
you just have to sneak another one.

Ella Cassidy (8)
St Vincent's RC Junior School, Altrincham

The Snail

In your garden you may find a snail
A slow, steady, slimy trail.
Slithering silently, cruising, never going fast
Choosing boggy, dark, damp ground
Where flowers and leaves abound
    Hard shell, smooth and round
    Trailing close to the ground
    Small home but very light
    Dark, damp places most of the time
    Horrible, silvery, glimmering slime.

Tom Pemberton (9)
St Vincent's RC Junior School, Altrincham

Hairdressers

What I hate about hairdressers is
sometimes they get in a habit of
hacking your hair.

What I like about hairdressers is
they straighten my hair
and it is fandabbydozi!

What I hate about hairdressers is
when they straighten my hair with the straightener
and it is very hot, it is like a little bit of fire.

What I like about hairdressers is
I like sitting on a high cushion.
It makes me feel like a teenager!

Ellie McAuliffe (7)
St Vincent's RC Junior School, Altrincham

A Lion Poem

I'm the king of the jungle,
I have a big roar.
I'm really fierce and
I've got lots of claws.
I eat lots of meat and
Then I'm hungry for more!
I creep up on animals
And take a big bite.
I feel very sleepy
When it's sunny and bright.
Then I wake up and play
In the middle of the night.

Harry Ford (9)
St Vincent's RC Junior School, Altrincham

School

What I hate about school is that
you have to do lots of work,
like maths and literacy.

What I like about school is that
you get lovely meals
at lunchtime.

What I hate about school is that
you get told off a lot
if you're naughty.

What I like about school is that
you get to go outside and play games,
like Top Trumps with your friends.

Isabella Langford (7)
St Vincent's RC Junior School, Altrincham

My Best Friends!

My best friends are always there for me.
Whenever I cut my knee they are there.
I fall asleep at night, they are in my dreams.
Their smile always *beams!*
Whenever you are feeling down or blue
They will come to help you.
They are sympathetic and *kind!*
They can sometimes read your mind.
They try and *help* all the time.
They are always smiling at me.
That is why my best friends are meant to be!

Lauren Reynolds (8)
St Vincent's RC Junior School, Altrincham

The Joys And Disappointments Of Food

What I hate about chips
is that even when I put a lot of vinegar on,
the chips absorb it and I can't taste the
delicious saltiness of the vinegar.

What I like about chicken nuggets
is that they go great with ketchup and they have
a lovely breadcrumb coating.

What I hate about potatoes
is they're so dry and the skin is so plain
and it takes ages to eat it on its own.

What I like about chocolate chip ice cream
is how it melts and the chocolate chips
are so crunchy.

Jamie Watkins (7)
St Vincent's RC Junior School, Altrincham

The Sea

What I hate about the sea is
that you can always step on very
sharp stones if you don't notice!

What I like about the sea is
when you can run into
the huge, wet waves!

What I hate about the sea is
how you can find dead creatures
and when you get soaked!

What I like about the sea is
how you can glide across
the salty waters!

Jennifer Robbins (7)
St Vincent's RC Junior School, Altrincham

My Stadium Underground

You can't see my football stadium, it's great,
but he can't see it, she can't and the baby can't.
My stadium is way below the ground
and you can slide down to get there.
There are no babies going wah - that is really loud,
All you can hear is the chanting of the crowd.
Also there are great players with a great manager - me,
The pitch is the best, that's all you can see.
You can even see the best, Pele and Beckham,
It has the biggest capacity in the world.
All of a sudden the crowd go dark - the other team score,
We gain one back and the crowd roar.
But the best thing is no one else knows about my stadium
under the ground.

Andrew Robbins (9)
St Vincent's RC Junior School, Altrincham

My Special Theme Park

You can't see my theme park, it is hidden underground
You can't hear it or find it, it doesn't make a sound
There you can land on the moon or create a big balloon.

There are lights all around you, you'll never be in the dark
It's fun, it's a classic and it's my theme park.

You can ride to Australia and jump on a kangaroo
And bounce and bounce all the night through.

All of a sudden our ride goes beep
We have to go because we have to sleep.

But the best thing is I named it, it's mine
Cos if you go there you will have a fab time.

Olivia Kelly (10)
St Vincent's RC Junior School, Altrincham

High Up Dreams

You can't see my dream world
because I made it all up.

My world is high up
right at the top of the sky.

There are no adults, school or homework.

Also there are sweets on trees
and money flowers.

You can do anything
and everyone is happy.

All of a sudden it rains
big, shiny diamonds.

But the best thing is
only kids go there.

Cara Dineen (9)
St Vincent's RC Junior School, Altrincham

Catz

There are lots of types of cats
Some with a loving for mats
Big and small
Tall and short
I love them all
Good and bad
Some that get mad
Prancing and jumping all around
They're sure to go where they're not allowed
I love them all.

Elizabeth Drabble (9)
St Vincent's RC Junior School, Altrincham

At The Bottom Of My Bed

You can't see the bottom of my bed,
Mum and Dad can't either,
Nor can my brother playing outside,
Lying under my quilt cosy and comfy.

My bed is in my bedroom, under my teddies,
Where no one goes but me,
Where all my special things will be.

There are no bad things about my room
Because there is a secret tomb,
So I always get what I want.

Also, there is a TV and an all that you can eat bar,
You can even see the latest movies when you want.

All of a sudden it disappears when anybody else comes in,
But the best thing is that nobody will know.

Laura Madden (9)
St Vincent's RC Junior School, Altrincham

School! School! School!

What I hate about school
is you have to be there on time.
What I like about school
is writing about art.
What I hate about school
is most of the playground is
covered in football players
and the way the other people
crash, bash and kaboom into you!
What I like about school
is how I can walk there
in three mini miniature minutes!
Cool isn't it?

Louis Pollitt (7)
St Vincent's RC Junior School, Altrincham

The Day The Zoo Escaped

The day the zoo escaped . . .

The slugs slid out slimily.
The eagles swooped out scarily.
The wolves chased out cheerfully,
The tortoise trembled out thankfully.
The hare hopped out happily.
The bears growled out grumpily.

Megan Fox (8)
St Vincent's RC Junior School, Altrincham

Fish Kennings

Scale shiner
Fast flapper
Bubble blower
Reed wrecker
Fine fins
Super swimmer
Ocean liver
Friday's dinner!

Declan Scopes (8)
St Vincent's RC Junior School, Altrincham

I See A Dog

It is leaping, sprinting and twisting.
It is moving its legs
Whitey, blondy and sparkling colours.
Thin and very slim.
Furry like inside a cushion.
It barks loudly like an engine.
It walks on its hind legs
And dashes like a dart.

Joe Mossop (8)
St Vincent's RC Junior School, Altrincham

The Day The Zoo Escaped

The day the zoo escaped . . .
The monkeys jumped out jaggedly,
The spiders scraped out scarily,
The tigers pounced out proudly,
The rabbits hopped out happily,
The rats sneaked out squeakily
The cheetah dashed out daringly,

But the sloth, sleepily, just hung around.

Bella Welsh (8)
St Vincent's RC Junior School, Altrincham

Spaghetti

What I hate about spaghetti is
it looks like worms.
What I like about spaghetti is
it twirls around your fork.
What I hate about spaghetti is
it always falls off your fork and it looks like slime.
What I like about spaghetti is
how it tickles on the way down to my tummy.

Samuel Chandler (7)
St Vincent's RC Junior School, Altrincham

Snakes

Snakes that slide, snakes that glide.
Snakes that are small, snakes that are tall.
Snakes that are colourful, snakes that are dull.
Each and every snake is different
But each and every snake is wonderful.

Michael Hoban (9)
St Vincent's RC Junior School, Altrincham

Football

What I hate about football is
when I get fouled.

What I like about football is
when I score a goal.

What I hate about football is
when I have to come off the pitch and be subbed.

What I like about football is
how I dribble the ball past people.

James Campion (7)
St Vincent's RC Junior School, Altrincham

The Day The Zoo Escaped

The day the zoo escaped . . .
The elephant pounced out proudly
The snake slithered out slickly
The parrot flew out flashily
The dog danced out dumbly
The hare hopped out happily,

But the sloth,
         sleepily,
                  just hung there.

Ella Mackenzie (8)
St Vincent's RC Junior School, Altrincham

Fiery

F lying sparks shining so bright
I n a blustery, cold winter's night
E ndless warmth around you
R ed, orange, yellow and blue
Y our flying sparks shining so bright.

Michael Doherty (8)
St Vincent's RC Junior School, Altrincham

Freddy The Fish

One day Freddy the fish was out for a swim
When suddenly something dreadful happened to him,
He swam in a net,
Which made him upset
Freddy the fish is now on a dish,
He made a big wish
That no fish would go for a swim
And have a dreadful thing
Happen to him.

Joseph O'Rourke (9)
St Vincent's RC Junior School, Altrincham

A Snake Poem

Snakes move quietly, sliding across the ground.
You sometimes don't know they are around.
Slippery and slimy, they can disguise.
Always waiting to surprise.
Snakes coil their bodies around their prey.
Always waiting throughout the day.
These reptiles live in water and on land.
Also sliding along the sand.

Phillip Ball (9)
St Vincent's RC Junior School, Altrincham

Stars!

Stars are wonderful, stars are bright,
They make me dance with sheer delight.
Stars are shiny, stars are fun,
They are pretty like the sun.
Stars make me jump, stars make me pounce,
They make me want to run, skip and bounce.

Olivia Gilbride (9)
St Vincent's RC Junior School, Altrincham

The Swimming Race

I'm taking part in a swimming race,
Will I win, do I have enough pace?
The boy at the side is coming up fast,
Is he behind or has he gone past?
I've touched the wall, I'm on my last length,
I wonder if I have any more strength?
The finish is in sight, I'm finally here,
I've won! I've won! Just listen to that cheer.

William Turner (9)
St Vincent's RC Junior School, Altrincham

I See A Horse

I see a horse
Skinny and golden.
Prancing around
Looking at me.
Giddy-up, giddy-up.
He runs through the field
With big green eyes
Looking at me.

Hannah Gallagher (8)
St Vincent's RC Junior School, Altrincham

The Day The Zoo Escaped

The day the zoo escaped . . .
The slug slid out slowly
The fox walked out proudly
The cheetah ran out scarily
The snake slid out slickly
The bears roared out loudly
The birds swooped out quickly
But the hippo stood where it was, quietly.

Jamie Pinkerton (8)
St Vincent's RC Junior School, Altrincham

Football

What I hate about football is
when they scream and shout.
What I like about football is
when I score a goal.
What I hate about football is
when I get hit on the head with the ball.
What I like about football is
how I tackle the other person.
What I hate about football is
when the other team score a goal.

Sean Joyce (7)
St Vincent's RC Junior School, Altrincham

Little Sisters

What I hate about little sisters
is when they copy you and annoy you.
What I like about little sisters
is that they are cute and pretend to be cute.
What I hate about little sisters
is that they whine and get their own ways
and pretend that they're ill but they're not.
What I like about little sisters
is how they cuddle you and play with you sweetly.

Olivia Hunter (7)
St Vincent's RC Junior School, Altrincham

Football Crazy

'England, England,' I hear my dad shout.
'Daddy, Daddy, it's time you took the dog out.'
Holly my dog is looking rather sad,
But Rooney has scored and my dad is glad.
England win and my dad grabs a beer,
Holly has seen nothing like it and shakes in fear!

Chloe Anne Murray (8)
St Vincent's RC Junior School, Altrincham

About A Dog

I see a dog
lying down at my feet.

Slow as a snail
black and soft.

Little tiny body
curly fur.

Barking noisily
brown shiny eyes

looking at me.

Nicola Scott (9)
St Vincent's RC Junior School, Altrincham

Elephant

Elephant
Squirting water
Stopping steadily
Grey, bumpy, flaky
Like a dinosaur
Rough and scary
Thundering and trumpeting
Knocked down trees
Mud roller
I love elephants!

Ben Houghton (8)
St Vincent's RC Junior School, Altrincham

Trees

The trees in the garden are very tall
And the ivy is growing up the wall
The baby plants are starting to bloom
In the hot sunshine during the afternoon.

Samantha Woodall (9)
St Vincent's RC Junior School, Altrincham

The Day The Zoo Escaped

The day the zoo escaped . . .
The snakes slithered out slickly,
The frog bounced out bouncily
The cheetah giggled out loudly
The elephants marched out happily
The rabbits hopped out carefully,
But the sloth,
      sleepily,
           just hung around.

Joanne Menon (8)
St Vincent's RC Junior School, Altrincham

Football

What I hate about football
is I can get badly hurt.
What I like about football
is I can get my team on the scoreboard.
What I hate about football
is being in goal and getting tripped up in the mud
then I get stood on.
What I like about football
is how my team can be really good.

Conor Perls (7)
St Vincent's RC Junior School, Altrincham

Belinda Bee

This is the tale of Belinda Bee who lived in a boat far out to sea,
The problem was no one could see Belinda was a very lonely bee.
So she took people sailing for a very small fee,
And the cabins needed their own private key.
She made a very nice cream tea,
The passengers said, 'How lucky are we!'

Catherine Keeling (9)
St Vincent's RC Junior School, Altrincham

I See a Guinea Pig

I see a guinea pig
sleeping soundly,
running speedily,
ginger and white,
round and small,
soft and cuddly,
rubbing away,
drinking and eating.
I see a guinea pig staring at me.

Henry Beverley (8)
St Vincent's RC Junior School, Altrincham

Beyond The Eye Can See

You can't see my dream world because it's mine.
My dream world is on a mystic island beyond the eye can see.
There are no rules so you can do anything you want.
Also there are money plants and chocolate plants.
You can travel in time backwards and forwards.
Right before your eyes something won't recognise something bright -
A palace glittering in the moonlight.
But the best thing is there's no school
So you can relax in this world!

Finn Pollitt (10)
St Vincent's RC Junior School, Altrincham

The Haunted House

A haunted house has creaky doors
With lots of spiders which crawl and crawl
All the floorboards are very creaky
Every movement seems very freaky
Anyone who comes in the haunted lair
At night all the ghosts come out to scare.

Rosie Gibb (9)
St Vincent's RC Junior School, Altrincham

Older Sisters

What I hate about older sisters
is that they think they're the boss.
What I like about older sisters
is if they're in a good mood they will help you with your homework.
What I hate about older sisters
is that they stay up really late and annoy you.
What I like about older sisters
is how they make you feel safe inside yourself.

Aoife Godfrey (7)
St Vincent's RC Junior School, Altrincham

Football

What I hate about football
is the way they give you a red card.
What I like about football
is the way I score.
What I hate about football
is the way they tackle me and score goals.
What I like about football
is how the teams are so prepared for matches.

Alexander Pemberton (7)
St Vincent's RC Junior School, Altrincham

Out Of This World Parents

It all started one night,
As I turned on the light.
My parents were at the door,
They were floating just off the floor.
Their bodies were green,
As green as a bean.
They danced and twirled,
Right out of this world.

Stephanie Anne Roberts (8)
St Vincent's RC Junior School, Altrincham

There Once Was A Witch Called Rowena

There once was a witch called Rowena
who couldn't have been any meaner,
her hair was bright green, her teeth were obscene
and her pet was a laughing hyena.
Rowena chased children off cliff tops,
she dive bombed old ladies at bus stops,
she conjured up spells that made toxic smells,
and made people reach for their eye drops.

Charlotte Simmons (9)
St Vincent's RC Junior School, Altrincham

My Cousin

What I hate about my cousin
is the way he fights with me.
What I like about my cousin
is when he lets me play on his PlayStation 2.
What I hate about my cousin
is when he doesn't let me play football in the garden.
What I like about my cousin
is when he plays with me.

Joseph Jones (7)
St Vincent's RC Junior School, Altrincham

What I Like And Hate

What I hate about my brother
is when he creeps up on me.
What I like about my brother
is the way he gives me a hug.
What I hate about my brother
is the way he shouts at me and the way he tells me off.
What I like about my brother
is how he tells me jokes.

Rebecca Connolly (7)
St Vincent's RC Junior School, Altrincham

Dog Kennings

A seat taker
A biscuit nicker
A dinner catcher
A stick chaser
A cat eater
A sea swimmer
A tree biter
A mud roller
A room ruiner.

Andrew Leyden (8)
St Vincent's RC Junior School, Altrincham

School!

What I hate about school
is the way you have to do loads of hard work.
What I love about school
is when you have golden time and play fun games.
What I hate about school
is when you get loads of homework and you have to be there on time.
What I love about school
is how you go swimming once a week, it's brill!

Elizabeth Sutton (7)
St Vincent's RC Junior School, Altrincham

The Day The Zoo Escaped

The day the zoo escaped
The donkeys galloped out beautifully
The ducks paddled out perfectly
The mice scurried out squeakily
The grasshoppers hopped out happily
The hyenas laughed out loudly
The birds soared out safely
But the lion just slept and snored.

Jennifer Kirton (8)
St Vincent's RC Junior School, Altrincham

Dog Kennings

Wood-chewer
Bone-eater
Cat-chaser
Cake-nicker
Back-scratcher
Toy-snatcher
Biscuit-lover
Bath-hater
Toe-kisser.

Danielle Humphreys-Woods (8)
St Vincent's RC Junior School, Altrincham

The Day The Zoo Escaped

The day the zoo escaped . . .
The parrot fluttered out fiercely.
The monkeys hung out happily.
The tigers pounced out powerfully.
The rats splattered out seriously.
The snakes slid out slickly.
The bear growled out grumpily.
The dog danced out dumbly.
But the sloth just hung around.

Liam Headd (8)
St Vincent's RC Junior School, Altrincham

My Secret Den

You can't see my den because it's hidden by boxes.
My den is under my bed.
There are no annoying people in my den.
Also there are lots of games.
You can even watch TV, at first it's really light.
All of a sudden it goes really dark.
But the best thing is that you can do what you want in my den.

Nathaniel Farrell (10)
St Vincent's RC Junior School, Altrincham

The Day The Zoo Escaped

The day the zoo escaped,
The horses raced out powerfully,
The bears stamped out slowly,
The camels walked out wearily,
The wolves howled out hauntedly,
The dolphins jumped out like jelly,
But the obedient zebra stared at them
Peacefully in her dream!

Trudy Akobeng (8)
St Vincent's RC Junior School, Altrincham

Dog Kennings

Shoe-shredder
Bed-nicker
Paw-printer
Best cardigan-ruiner
Olympic-runner
Cat-chaser
Food-scoffer
Teacup-smasher.

Megan Lewis (8)
St Vincent's RC Junior School, Altrincham

Dogs

Bed snatcher,
Bacon eater,
Playful fetcher,
Barking shouter,
Mud roller,
Car snatcher,
Garden ruiner,
Quick panter.

Emma Phelan (8)
St Vincent's RC Junior School, Altrincham

My Sister And I

What I hate about my sister
is the way that she doesn't want to kiss me.
What I like about my sister
is the way she plays imaginary games with me.
What I hate about my sister
is the way that she tells on me and she doesn't include me
in games when her friends are round.
What I like about my sister
is how she really gets scared when she sees a pretend spider.

Elliot Malley (7)
St Vincent's RC Junior School, Altrincham

My Best Mate With A Cold

I see a black dog barking at me,
Charging at me.
He is black with a bit of white on him.
His body is a smaller version of a cow.
His fur is soft and cuddly and dark black.
He makes a growling sort of noise,
And he mooches around the garden.
He is sneezing at me.

Andrew Cartledge (9)
St Vincent's RC Junior School, Altrincham

The Day The Zoo Escaped

The day the zoo escaped,
The wolves walked out wonderingly,
The slugs slid out slyly,
The hares hopped out happily,
The tortoises trembled out thinkingly,
The parrots piped out playfully,
The snakes slithered out slowly,
But the goat, feeling grumpy, just hung about.

Megan Quigley (8)
St Vincent's RC Junior School, Altrincham

The Story Of Mary

There was once a lady named Mary,
She travelled to Tipperary,
She went on her bike,
Instead of her trike.
Now people did say she looked funny,
When she called everybody her 'Honey'.
One day there was a crash
But none other than a bash
And that was the end of Mary,
The one who was incredibly scary.

Francine Gilmore (9)
St Vincent's RC Junior School, Altrincham

Ponies

Thoroughbreds, Arabs, cobs and all
Even Shetlands that are really small
They go to the field and get all muddy
Some come back really grubby
Some are cheeky, some are bad
Some are happy, some are sad
I love horses, they're the best
Now it's night, they're all at rest.

Hannah Crowther (9)
St Vincent's RC Junior School, Altrincham

Bouncing

Bouncing, bouncing everywhere
On my bed and down the stairs.
Bouncing, bouncing everywhere
On a pogo stick in the air
Bouncing, bouncing with a ball
I hope I don't trip and fall
Bouncing.

Connor Murphy (9)
St Vincent's RC Junior School, Altrincham

My Sister

When my sister was born,
She was as pink as a prawn.

After a while
She grew a big smile.

Mum changed her diapers the most.
You wouldn't want to get too close.

If you know what I mean
You wouldn't be too clean.

When she screams, Dad says, 'Give it a rest.'
But I don't care she's still the best!

William Goddard (8)
St Vincent's RC Junior School, Altrincham

The Scary Closet

You can't see my spooky room,
My closet is at the bottom of my room.
There are no toys in my closet, just a box,
And in the box is a book of all my dreams.
Also there are two candles and a skeleton guarding it,
And whenever I read the book it gives me good luck.
You can even put your hand right through it.
All of a sudden every midnight the book disappears,
But the best thing is no one can see it but me.

Jasmine McGovern (9)
St Vincent's RC Junior School, Altrincham

There Once Was A Spider Called Fred

There once was a spider called Fred
He lived in my grandma's shed
He made his home working to the bone
So that he could be fed.

Catching flies in his large web
An old plant pot for his bed
Working all day, playing away
Until he got squashed, *dead!*

Lorna Berry (9)
St Vincent's RC Junior School, Altrincham

The Octopus Called Tim

There once was an octopus called Tim,
He lived in water but he could not swim.
His body was as green as grass,
His legs were as glossy as glass.

One day he ventured out of safe seas,
He met a shark who was hard to please.
The shark grabbed Tim and his jaws went crunch,
Tim became that greedy shark's lunch!

Charlotte Malley (9)
St Vincent's RC Junior School, Altrincham

Children!

I look at the children playing in the town.
Some of them laugh, some of them frown.
Some on the slide, some on the swings.
They shout at the birds flapping their wings.
Along comes Rover wagging his tail
Barking at the boats as they set sail.
Off goes Rover down the street
His owner goes to buy some meat.
Darkness comes, it's the end of the day
It's time for children to finish their play.
'Come inside and go to bed,' their mother said.
Within a blink of an eye they were resting their heads.

Lauren Sheppard (9)
St Vincent's RC Junior School, Altrincham

The Day The Zoo Escaped . . .

The rabbits hopped out happily
The snake slid out slickly
The elephant pounced out proudly
The tortoise walked out weakly
The dog danced out daringly
The rats sneaked out secretly
    But the sloth
    Sleepily
    Just hung around.

Beth Fielding (8)
St Vincent's RC Junior School, Altrincham

My Underground Hideout

You can't see my underground hideout because only I know
                                                where it is.
My underground hideout is under my garden but it's very big.
There are no people to boss me about in my base because
                                                I am the boss.
Also there are 26 quad bikes and 9 massive monster truck areas.
All of a sudden when you enter, lots of bright lights turn on one by one.
But the best thing is if you stand next to the tree in my garden,
And type in a code a door opens and you slide down a big slide
                                                to enter.

Joshua Boland (9)
St Vincent's RC Junior School, Altrincham

My Old Cousin

What I hate about my cousin
is he's always controlling my computer.
What I like about my cousin
is the way he makes cool models.
What I hate about my cousin
is the way he scares me out of my pants
and I fall over!
What I like about my cousin
is how he gets in a big, dirty old strop.
Best thing about him is,
he's got a good sense of humour.

Patrick Doyle (8)
St Vincent's RC Junior School, Altrincham

Spiders

What I hate about spiders
is when they crawl up your back.

What I like about spiders
is when they come down into the bath
and my sisters *scream*.

What I hate about spiders
is when the spiders go down my back
and it tickles.

What I like about spiders
is how they spin webs.

Joseph Burns (7)
St Vincent's RC Junior School, Altrincham

Cat Kennings

Fur licker,
Bird watcher,
Mice eater,
Garden lover,
Mat lover,
Dog hater,
Fish starer,
Sleep lover,
Human lover.

Joshua Edwards (8)
St Vincent's RC Junior School, Altrincham

Climbing Frame

Hanging upside down
Feeling funny
Feeling sick
Pulling funny faces
Blue sky
Sandy floor
Moving
Up and down
Hanging on with elbows
And one foot
Children
Screaming
And shouting
What fun!

Michael Arnold (8)
Wistaston Junior School

Climbing Frame

I'm touching the sky
As cold as steel.
Feels like cotton wool,
Looks like
The deep blue sea.
Feeling glad I'm high,
Ice cream truck,
Loads of children.
Children screaming,
Shouting and yelling,
Freedom.

Alice Capper (7)
Wistaston Junior School

Climbing Frame

Clouds puffed
With rain
I smiled to the
Sky above me
So bright and blue
Hot sun
White sun
Climbing frame
Hot
Feel happy
Upside down
High up
Children play
Below me
Sun shines above
Bars all around me
No parents
Free.

Daniel Burgess (7)
Wistaston Junior School

Animal Year

Summer is like a snake,
Slithering across the sandy beach.

Spring is a monkey,
Swinging on a tree.

Winter is a ghost,
Saying . . . 'Boohhh!'

Autumn is a caterpillar,
Crawling up a tree.

Melissa Ford (7)
Wistaston Junior School

The Climbing Frame

Children holding onto the bars
Bright blue sky
The frame is yellow
They climb to the sky
Feeling like they can swing free
No school, no work
Above the bars they laugh and scream
Lots of sweets and chocolate
Weather is cold
Children shout and whisper
Nice holidays
They tell secrets
Burning golden sun
Screaming and laughing children
They climb to the sky
Drinks and food are nice
Below the frame they walk about
Smelly people wonder about
Good and naughty children
Sensible and stupid
Kind and nice.

Ryan Cooper (7)
Wistaston Junior School

Apple

Round and shiny red
Big and heavy
Juicy and hard
Smells juicy
And sweet
It leaves my mouth feeling nice and sweet.

Sophie Winby (7)
Wistaston Junior School

Climbing Frame

Hanging children
Upside down
Slight wind
Blowing through clothes
Sun shining
Hot and bright
Glorious blue sky
No ground in sight
Climbing to the very top
Sitting down
Clinging on tight
Or lazing around
Children screaming
And smiling
Feeling brave
Or scared
Excited.

Lewis George (7)
Wistaston Junior School

Summer

Summer is like a cow,
Mooing in the field,
Waiting to be milked.
Summer drinks in the milk . . .
Out of the cow.
Making it healthy,
And strong.
Always
Drinking
Milk
In the fresh morning.

Amy Davies (7)
Wistaston Junior School

Opposite Feelings

Happiness is an amber glow flickering from the open hearth.
It sounds like busy birds singing peacefully
in the morning summer sun.
Happiness tastes like ruby-red, succulent strawberries,
ready and ripe to tickle my taste buds.
It smells like smiling sunflowers swiftly dancing in the gentle breeze.
Happiness feels like a newborn kitten's fleecy fur, soft and smooth.

Anger is scarlet-red like witches' potions raging, bubbling,
spraying in their cauldrons.
It sounds like a piece of chalk screeching across a blackboard
making you wince inside.
Anger tastes like toxic waste climbing down your throat,
sour and sticky.
It smells like an unknown gas making your head spin like a hurricane,
choking you slowly . . . slowly.
Anger feels like bleach making me itch all over,
dressed in a deadly bright red rash.

Eleanor Cresswell (10)
Wistaston Junior School

Emotions

Fear tastes as strong as extra strong mints.
Excited feels like just getting on a plane to go on holiday.
Fear feels as rough as a rock.
Excited sounds like a merry-go-round which never stops.
Fears looks like the inside of a ghost train.
Excited looks like a big wave rising towards you.
Fear looks like a thunderstorm lashing against the windows.
Excited tastes like home-made choc chip muffins coming
                                        out of the oven.
Fear smells like rotten potatoes from their bag.
Excited smells like you are getting nearer and nearer to the sea.

Zoe Venables (10)
Wistaston Junior School

Climbing Frame

Children are climbing
Screaming children
Laughing children
Worried children
Excited children
Swinging for their lives
Hanging upside down
Swinging for dares
For money
Bodies swinging
Above the ground
Swaying
Wind gently blowing
Clouds slowly
Moving like a tortoise
Sky-blue as the summer sea
Feeling free.

Jack Baskerville (8)
Wistaston Junior School

Apple

Smooth, dotted,
Almost round and stripy.
Light and rough,
Cold and bumpy.
Orange, fresh, fruity and nice.
Juicy, rough and watery.
It tastes like grapes.
It leaves my mouth feeling watery, fresh and cold.

Lucy Skellon (7)
Wistaston Junior School

Different Emotions!

Excitement is scorching crimson like a whizzing roller coaster.
It sounds like a Caribbean festival parading in the evening sunlight.
Tastes like a juicy bright mango stinging my lips.
It smells like a rich dark chocolate bar melting in the warmth
                                        of my mouth.
Feels like a volcano erupting slowly, spilling smoky ashes,
                                        swirling in the wind.
Reminds me of pink flamingos flapping on the banks of the long river.

Anger is a shadowy black, like a dim-lighted cave.
It sounds like one hundred tigers roaring and scratching.
Anger tastes like a sickening poison bubbling in my mouth.
Smells like a burning blaze destroying everything in sight.
Feels like battering green goblins leaping about causing
                                        endless trouble!

Georgia Owen (10)
Wistaston Junior School

Anger

Anger is a scarlet burning flame roasting and toasting all in sight.
It tastes like the hottest curry of all demolishing my taste buds
                                        as it passes.
Anger sounds like a cackling, aged witch carrying a screaming,
                                        bubbly potion.
It feels like a mysterious monster sucking out my soul leaving
                                        me dumbstruck with horror.
Anger reminds me of a cheetah charging at their helpless
                        and defenceless prey, roaring and excited.

Rebecca Cooper (10)
Wistaston Junior School

Bubbling Excitement And Silent Nervousness

Excitement is fizzing purple, jumping and laughing.
It sounds like bubbling water trickling like a wonderful waterfall.
Excitement tastes like sherbet, tangy and sour on the tip
of your tongue.
A smell drifts through the door of boiling sweets, humming cheerfully
on the metal pan.
Excitement feels like popping bubbles gliding, glistening in the air.
Reminding me of the shimmering, shining sun cart-wheeling joyfully
back and forth.
Nervousness is white, thinking about whether to move its wispy body
forward or not.
Nervousness bites its nails, its teeth chattering and battering together.
It's very quiet, someone fish-mouthing a song in an echoing hall.
It tastes like spaghetti getting tangled up in your throat.
Nervousness, smelling like nothing, like it is not there at all,
silent and still.

Hollie Chapman (10)
Wistaston Junior School

Excitement

Excitement is like an FA Cup final when your home town is playing,
It sounds like a dog's running footsteps bombing forwards
to be patted.
It tastes like a raspberry whirl ice cream ready to be lashed
and devoured.
It smells like a hot stew sizzling, bubbling in the corner fire inviting
you to slurp at it,
It feels like water slithering on my body and soothing in my hair,
It reminds me of when I met my friends.

Adam Done (10)
Wistaston Junior School

Fierce Anger

Anger is the colour blood-red bubbling up inside me,
My head nearly exploding in rage.

It tastes like red-hot chilli pepper sauce,
One drop turns my face maroon-red,
Like a deadly poison.

It smells like smoke from a raging fire
Burning and suffocating everything in sight.

Anger sounds like a mighty lion roaring,
Sending chills down the spine of its innocent prey.

Anger feels like a tight, itchy, prickly jumper
Hugging my bare skin on a hot summer's day.

Danielle Baskerville (10)
Wistaston Junior School

Climbing Frame

Blazing sky shining
Children
Death defying acts
Clinging for dear life
Hands harder than metal
Feels like
Touching the sky
Opposite is the sky slide
Wind brushing their hair
Free parents
Children's blood
Goes to their head.

Kyle Woolrich (7)
Wistaston Junior School

The Squirrel

In winter the squirrel eats acorns
As he hibernates.
His house a cold hole
In a tree.
He sleeps until winter is finished.
Spring comes,
He wakes up
Into a brand new day.

Isabelle Backs (7)
Wistaston Junior School

Apple

Round, shiny, small, red and green, and spotted.
Smooth and light, cold and rough.
It smells sweet and fruity.
Tastes of grapes and juicy.
It leaves my mouth feeling soft.

Abigail Oldham (7)
Wistaston Junior School

The Summer Snake

A snake arrives in a scorching desert,
Where he waits for his food.
He waits in the summer
He never stops waiting for his food
He finds a mouse
He swallows it whole.

Nicola Parker (7)
Wistaston Junior School

Summer

Summer is like an elephant
Squirting water
On his back
To cool him down
Rolling in the mud
To get muddy
So he can squirt more water
On his hot back.

Jeremy Griffiths (7)
Wistaston Junior School

Happiness

Happiness is like a sunny day.
Happiness is like it is Christmas Day when you wake up in bed.
Happiness is like a cat miaowing all day.
Happiness smells like a bright, new morning.
Happiness sounds like the birds whistling all day on the beach.
Happiness tastes like chocolate cake on my birthday.

Jake Williamson (10)
Wistaston Junior School

Summer

Katie the kangaroo hops madly through
The scorching, swishing sun,
Hoping to find some fresh, cool,
Relaxing water to drink.
She plays with elephants in the boiling,
Swishy, soft sea.
Soon she calms down
And goes home ready for autumn.

Molly Evans (7)
Wistaston Junior School

Autumn

Kangaroos bouncing
Like the conkers
Falling off the trees
In autumn
Leaves turn brown
Like the kangaroos.

Harry Young (7)
Wistaston Junior School

Happiness

Happiness sounds like calm music
Happiness looks like snow at Christmas
Happiness tastes like vanilla ice cream
Happiness smells like a birthday cake
Happiness feels like a smooth ball.

Ben Jones (10)
Wistaston Junior School

Summer

Giraffes love to eat
The leaves off the tall trees
They absolutely love to sunbathe
In the hot summer sun
They lie waiting for food
Glad to be giraffes.

Alexander Alton (7)
Wistaston Junior School

Climbing Frame

Children are playing
having fun.
They are feeling
the cold silver bars
hanging like bananas
on a banana tree.
Above them are
pieces of chewing gum clouds,
near the deep blue sky.
Below are other
children laughing
giggling like a bear.

Megan Minshull (7)
Wistaston Junior School

The Great Bear

The bear in the night he rustles in the bin
Trying to find food in the dark
Then he smells man, quickly he hides
He sniffs again
Food!
He finds it
He eats.

George Galanis (7)
Wistaston Junior School

Apple

Smooth and light
Smooth and hard like a stone
Smells like perfume
Tastes like grapes
It leaves my mouth feeling soft.

Chloe Hutchings (7)
Wistaston Junior School

Monday's Child

Monday's child looks an ugly sight
Tuesday's child is not very bright
Wednesday's child collects music stickers
Thursday's child wets her knickers
Friday's child sucks its hair
Saturday's child can't sit on a chair
And the child that is born on the seventh day
Is a pain in the neck - like the rest OK?

Christopher Wright (8)
Wistaston Junior School

Apple

It's dotted and bright red.
The stalk is brown.
It is red and green.
It's cold and rough.
It smells like blackcurrant.
It tastes of apple juice.
It leaves my mouth feeling wet.

Alasdair Johnstone (7)
Wistaston Junior School

Spring

The people trampling on the dry earth
Spring is looming
It lies there waiting
For the heat of summer
Coming when spring . . .
                          Dies.

Liam Morris (7)
Wistaston Junior School

Winter

In the winter a hedgehog lived in an old lady's garden
She was blind with a guide dog called Bruno
Before his nap he went for a run in the garden
He saw the hedgehog
He brought the old lady to see the hedgehog
She called her neighbours
They called the RSPCA
Who saved him.

Sebastian Davies (7)
Wistaston Junior School

Apple

It is very smooth
And cold
It is heavy
Smells juicy
It tastes like apple juice
It leaves my mouth feeling soft.

Victoria Cohoon (7)
Wistaston Junior School

Spring

The mighty dragon breathes
The mighty air in and out
Out of his cave
Out of hibernation
Looking for food
In the cold, cold air.

Cameron Ledwards (7)
Wistaston Junior School

Young Writers - Once Upon A Rhyme Poems From Cheshire

Apple

Round, all colours like red, green and yellow
Bumpy skin with a stalk and pips
Skin is smooth, soft and strong
Thick and cold
Like stone
Fresh flowers
It leaves my mouth feeling sweet.

Marcus West (7)
Wistaston Junior School

Sunshine The Cat

In summer
Sunshine goes out to sunbathe
By the paddling pool
The children are playing in the paddling pool
Under the scorching sun
'Miaow! Purr! Purr!'

Katie Davies (7)
Wistaston Junior School

Apple

Red and white spots
Round
Light, cold and slippery
Smells like a fruit perfume
Juicy, fruity
Leaves my mouth feeling sad.

Hannah Mann (7)
Wistaston Junior School

Excitement

Excitement is a baby-blue blanket ready to be cuddled,
It sounds like a stampede of elephants being chased by lions,
It smells like the smoke of your own birthday cake getting
closer and closer,
And feels like you're dropping down a roller coaster, weightlessly.
It tastes like a piece of white chocolate slithering down
your throat, yummy!
Excitement looks like warthogs on unicycles, cycling the tightrope.

Zachary Thomas (10)
Wistaston Junior School

Anger

Anger is scarlet like a burning furnace.
It reminds me of war as the bombs and missiles trample
through countries destroying everything.
Anger smells like smoke floating off the top of flames.
It feels like a door fiercely closing on your hand.
Anger looks like the fearless face on a fighting tiger.

Jessica Saunders (10)
Wistaston Junior School

All About Fear

Fear is seeing a spider in your bedroom.
Fear is seeing a sprout on your plate.
Fear is seeing a pile of homework in your bag.
Fear is going to a new school on your own.
Fear is when you have to go to Asda food shopping.
Fear is when you have to do a performance on stage.

Lauren Benson (10)
Wistaston Junior School

Excitement

Excitement is pale orange like a hot boiling pot of soup
on the red-hot stove swirling as it cooks.
It tastes like red-hot chilli peppers sizzling as they jump up and down.
It sounds like someone getting into a relaxing, hot tub.
Excitement reminds me of playing with my friendly,
happy and joyful friends.
It feels like scoring a brilliant goal from the halfway line.
It smells like a hot stew bubbling in the pot.

Ben Minshull (10)
Wistaston Junior School

Anger

Anger is scarlet like a raging furnace about to explode.
It sounds like a vicious predator ready to attack its helpless victims.
Anger's chilli taste burns inside the mouth.
It smells like the deadly, choking smoke from a fierce fire.
Anger feels like boiling lava spilling down the volcano.
It reminds me of a tiger racing after its victim, turning every corner
ready to devour it.

Emma Hay (10)
Wistaston Junior School

Happiness

Happiness is orange like the warm summer sun.
It sounds like birds twittering in the trees, contented.
Happiness is creamy, soft ice cream melting in my mouth.
It smells like flowers dancing in the breeze.
Happiness beams in the distance.
It reminds me of pale pink buds waltzing in the cool wind.
Happiness feels like the fur on a playful puppy, smooth and soft.

Lucy-Kate Jones (11)
Wistaston Junior School

Evil

Evil is grey like big rain clouds ready to burst on a lonely traveller.
It sounds like a broken violin screeching down your earholes.
Evil tastes like sour grapes, bitter and sharp.
It feels like peppercorns that haven't been ground, scorching
                                                    your tongue.
Evil smells like thick black clouds of toxic waste billowing out of
                                                    exhaust pipes.
It reminds me of a scheming witch planning her revenge on
                                                    her next victim.

Georgina Gargan (10)
Wistaston Junior School

Happiness Feelings

Happiness is amber like a strutting sun trying to find its way
through the patchy clouds.
It sounds like the summer's sun is singing joyfully.
It tastes like soft, juicy peaches waiting to tickle my taste buds.
It smells as if a rosebud is about to pop open like a spring.
It feels like newborn chicks all fluffy and warm twisting and turning
waiting for their mums to feed them.
It reminds me of a light pink blanket waiting for a newborn baby
to sleep on it.

Amy Wrench (10)
Wistaston Junior School

Anger

Anger is scarlet like a furious furnace
It sounds like thunder lighting the sky
Anger is a hot chilli curry burning your throat
It smells like rubbish from a dump, like diesel that's never been used
Anger feels like rough, stiff sandpaper silently scraping through
                                                    the night
It reminds you about vicious memories, a mystery never to be found.

Simon Scott (10)
Wistaston Junior School

Opposite Emotions

Anger is scarlet like a raging furnace.
It sounds like lightning crashing and smashing.
Anger, it's a bitter taste that can't be washed away.
It smells like smoke whooshing from dragons' ears in rage,
swiftly spreading itself.
Anger feels like a bulging earthquake shaking fiercely,
making me tremble.
It reminds me of bulls digging their hooves into the ground,
charging non-stop, pounding at one panic-stricken person.

Happiness is banana split, yellow like chirping Easter chicks
dancing with joy.
It tastes like silky butter melting slowly into your toast.
Happiness sounds like the swaying of smiling sunflowers.
It feels like strands of fluff on a baby panda, soft and smooth.
It smells like lipgloss pink candyfloss, sweet and sugary.
Happiness reminds me of snow, snow falling gently
ready to be made into pompom snowballs.

Nicolé Dykes (10)
Wistaston Junior School

Madness

Madness, rainbow colours spit from smashed glass in confusion.
It sounds like a cacophony of barking dogs annoying the neighbours.
It tastes like sour sweets tingling your tongue,
making your face change.
It smells like smoke swirling, twirling in a confused daze.
Madness feels like a spitting furnace scolding the air.
It reminds me of a crazed bull charging like a thousand soldiers
after their target.

James Briscoe (10)
Wistaston Junior School

Anger

Anger is crimson like a smoky heart burning in passion,
Anger pounds its hooves across your scalp, digging in its claws
as it passes . . . passes by.
It tastes like tangy lemons burning your taste buds.
Anger, a whiff of smoking cigar peeping its head round
the corner of the room you are in.
His clenched fist scarlet in rage, a trapped howling wolf.
It reminds me of a missile lined up and thundering
as it pounds towards its prey like a leopard, eager.

Emily Davies (10)
Wistaston Junior School

Anger

Anger burns scarlet, a furious furnace.
It sounds like heavy footsteps thumping louder and louder.
The taste of anger wells up inside your throat, filling your mouth,
Anger looks like a beast lashing out and swiping its claws
across a hunter, roaring.
It feels like someone constantly stabbing you
and the pain will never go.

Leo Davies (10)
Wistaston Junior School

Apple

Dotted and round.
Cold and smooth and heavy.
Smells juicy like my mum's favourite perfume
And like blackcurrant.
It tastes like orange.
It leaves my mouth feeling sweet.

Joshua Ollier (7)
Wistaston Junior School

Anger

Anger is scarlet like a raging volcano erupting in the black of the night.
It sounds like a monstrous thunderstorm ready to destroy
all of Earth's creations.
Anger tastes like a sour lemon squirting onto defenceless gums.
It smells like a smoking cloud of fumes swirling and twirling
into the bright blue clear sky.
Anger reminds me of when my sister gobbles all my sweets.

Sophie Hulme (10)
Wistaston Junior School

Happiness

Happiness is Caribbean flowers dancing in the wind to and fro.
Happiness is a gentle hum as the sun raises over the meadow
through the long grass like there's not a care in the world.
Happiness is a tingling taste that sizzles your tongue,
The taste dancing like there's a parade going down your throat.
Happiness is a smooth surface, warm and cuddly
like a friendly teddy bear.
Happiness is a luscious red rose, a beautiful scented fume.

Sam Brierley (10)
Wistaston Junior School

Happiness

Happiness is pink like gentle, delicate rose petals.
It sounds like the hummingbird sweetly whistling a tune.
Happiness tastes like melting chocolate tingling my taste buds.
It smells like roses' rich perfume floating in the wind.
Happiness looks like robins hopping on branches in the warm breeze.
It feels like the fluffy hair on a rabbit as they play, contented.
Happiness reminds me of puppies chasing each other on the swaying
grass in the fields.

Saskia Chery (10)
Wistaston Junior School

Climbing Frame

I see children.
Frame is huge.
Weather is sunny.
Feeling happy.
Want a good grip.
Bars are hot.
Hot, burning, golden sun.
Above is the sky.
Below is the ground.
Near are our friends.
Opposite is my mum.
Bright blue sky.
Bright white clouds.

Hayley Parry (7)
Wistaston Junior School

Summer

Summer is like a lovely lamb hopping
in the lovely, sweet grass.
She tumbles and grumbles
in the scorching sun.
After all that she is joyful!

Chloe Hill (7)
Wistaston Junior School

Happiness

Happiness is butter-yellow smeared over hot toast in the morning.
It sounds like laughing and playing in the beaming sun.
The lovely, sweet, golden honey tastes like silk floating in your mouth.
It smells of daffodils dancing round and round.
Happiness feels like a loveable rabbit springing up and down.

Laura Averill (10)
Wistaston Junior School

Fear

Fear is when you're trapped in a haunted house.
Fear is a smelly sewer
Fear tastes like an old, rotten apple
Fear sounds like a robber coming towards you
Fear is like a rough brick wall.

Thomas Davies (10)
Wistaston Junior School

Summer

Cheetahs running in the sun,
Splashing in water, having fun.
Ripping red meat,
Life is sweet.

Philip Hellon (7)
Wistaston Junior School

Summer

The beavers are always in the pool
Splashing every day
Sunbathing with the bright sun
Heating up his brown skin
Diving off a big rock.

Daniel Wakeham (7)
Wistaston Junior School

Angry

Angry was like seeing a tornado running towards me.
Angry was as loud as a tractor.
Angry was when I heard my alarm clock.,
Angry was like seeing homework.
Angry was like seeing a tidal wave causing devastation.

James Astbury (11)
Wistaston Junior School

Apple

Round with stalks
Red
Small, cold and heavy
Smooth like a pig and juicy
It leaves my mouth feeling sweet.

William Brown (7)
Wistaston Junior School

Summer

Summer is a squirrel
Running up a tree
Hiding from people
Staying till they've gone
Scampering down to play with their friends.

Sophie Jones (7)
Wistaston Junior School

Apple

Red, spotty and round
Soft, hard and light
Juicy, fresh and sweet
Crunchy and sweet
It leaves my mouth sticky.

Jazmin Leitch-Smith (8)
Wistaston Junior School

Summer

A dragon sunbathing on the beach,
Breathing fire at the villagers.
Hot as the sun
Burning down.

Charlie Taylor (7)
Wistaston Junior School

Anger

Anger is a crimson red like Hell's mischief-maker,
It tastes like red-hot lava scolding your tongue,
Eardrums pop at the ridiculous rage of the beast,
It reminds me of an earthquake striking a cramped city,
It feels like you have the power to crush a building
with your bare hands,
It smells like a burning fire in a dusty, old paper mill,
weaving its way through the building.

Oliver Gibbs-Murray (10)
Wistaston Junior School

Happiness

Happiness looks like a rainbow shining in the sky.
Happiness smells like beautiful flowers in all kinds of colours.
Happiness is a summer holiday, walking on the silky beach
                                    in the sprinkling sun.
Happiness sounds as calm as a sunset dinner over a tropical night.
Happiness tastes like the biggest ice cream in the world.
Happiness feels as pretty as me!

Katie Bennion (10)
Wistaston Junior School

Anger

Anger is like a thunderstorm rising in the air
Anger smells like burnt toast
Anger feels like you get sick and never wake up and have been
                                    asleep for ages
It sounds like a thunderstorm hitting us with a tremendous crash
Anger tastes like rotten eggs
Anger looks like someone punching the door and hurting themselves.

Stacey Parry (10)
Wistaston Junior School

Climbing Frame

Children screaming and laughing.
Shining metal bars,
hot under little fingers,
Under a boiling,
hot, golden sun.
Feeling happy and carefree.
Screaming,
shouting,
want a cool ice cream?
Below is a frog,
jumping slowly.
Above are candyfloss clouds.
Near are sweet,
beautiful flowers.
Opposite is my mum,
waving and wafting.

Josh Leitch-Smith (8)
Wistaston Junior School

Climbing Frame

I see clouds up high.
Hot weather.
Feeling excited.
Below are flowers
that glow in the dark.
Above
some blackbirds
flying high.
Trees are
rustling loudly.
Children laughing
upside down.

Chloé Clarke (7)
Wistaston Junior School

Nerves

Red-hot is nerves.
Nerves are butterflies in your stomach.
Sitting an exam makes you feel nervous.
Nerves are like sitting on a roller coaster waiting for it to drop.
Nerves are truths lurking in your mind.
Nerves is when the electric goes out and you're home alone.
Nerves is a hurricane rampaging towards you.

James Hankey (10)
Wistaston Junior School

Anger

Anger is a troll rampaging through a school of innocent children.
Anger sounds like a lion bellowing its mighty roar.
It tastes like a super sour, rotten apple.
It smells like a 200-year-old rotten cabbage and cream.
It feels like a thunderstorm striking inside your head.
Anger looks like a black hole of never-ending frustration.

Matthew Higson (10)
Wistaston Junior School

Apple

Spotty, stalk,
Green and rough,
Round and shiny,
Soft and bruised,
Juicy, sweet and fresh,
Crunchy and sweet,
It leaves my mouth feeling sticky.

Amy Young (7)
Wistaston Junior School

Anger

Anger smells like old, rotten socks,
Anger looks like a thunderstorm in the midnight sky,
Anger feels like a rough brick wall,
Anger sounds like the brakes on a motorbike,
Anger tastes like a bitter lemon.

Rebecca Small (11)
Wistaston Junior School

Fear

Fear smells like a cow's muck on a farm.
Fear is like walking through a graveyard at midnight alone.
Fear feels like a big cobweb in a spooky cave.
Fear sounds like a horror movie and you're in it.
Fear tastes like more of school's meals.

Ross Need (10)
Wistaston Junior School

Fear . . .

Fear looks like toxic waste bubbling in its barrel.
Fear sounds like shattering glass.
Fear feels like when you dive in freezing water.
Fear tastes like a sour lemon.

James Parker (10)
Wistaston Junior School

Angry

Angry is like a thunderstorm coming towards us.
Anger is like a drum being hit.
Angry is like a giant looking for something to eat.
Angry is like someone turning the radio up full blast.

Joe-Axl Buchanan-Bible (10)
Wistaston Junior School

Happiness

Happiness is like a lolly in a heat wave.
Happiness is like Christmas Day with snow.
Happiness is the smell of home-made chocolate cake.
It tastes as cold as ice cream.
It looks like a million smiles.
Happiness sounds like laughter.
Happiness feels like you have won the lottery.
Happiness feels like lying on sand on the beach.

Laura Johnstone (10)
Wistaston Junior School

Fear

Fear is a mouse running like a jet from a cat
Fear is when you feel a hairy spider crawling across your face
Fear smells like sour milk that has been out of date for weeks
Fear sounds like nails scraping on a blackboard
Fear is when you smell rotten eggs
Fear is when you see a hurricane storming towards you.

Reece Hardstaff (11)
Wistaston Junior School

Anger

Anger smells of 200-year-old milk
Anger sounds like a thunderstorm stamping towards me
Anger feels like an electric shock
Anger tastes like stale eggs
Anger sounds like hard rock music
Anger tastes like the bitter and sourest lemon ever
Anger looks like my teacher's face when I bought my homework in late.

Jessica Hassall (10)
Wistaston Junior School